STRATEGIC INFORMATION SECURITY

OTHER AUERBACH PUBLICATIONS

The ABCs of IP Addressing
Gilbert Held
ISBN: 0-8493-1144-6

The ABCs of LDAP
Reinhard Voglmaier
ISBN: 0-8493-1346-5

The ABCs of TCP/IP
Gilbert Held
ISBN: 0-8493-1463-1

Building an Information Security Awareness Program
Mark B. Desman
ISBN: 0-8493-0116-5

Building a Wireless Office
Gilbert Held
ISBN: 0-8493-1271-X

The Complete Book of Middleware
Judith Myerson
ISBN: 0-8493-1272-8

Computer Telephony Integration, 2nd Edition
William A. Yarberry, Jr.
ISBN: 0-8493-1438-0

Electronic Bill Presentment and Payment
Kornel Terplan
ISBN: 0-8493-1452-6

Information Security Architecture
Jan Killmeyer Tudor
ISBN: 0-8493-9988-2

Information Security Management Handbook, 4th Edition, Volume 1
Harold F. Tipton and Micki Krause, Editors
ISBN: 0-8493-9829-0

Information Security Management Handbook, 4th Edition, Volume 2
Harold F. Tipton and Micki Krause, Editors
ISBN: 0-8493-0800-3

Information Security Management Handbook, 4th Edition, Volume 3
Harold F. Tipton and Micki Krause, Editors
ISBN: 0-8493-1127-6

Information Security Management Handbook, 4th Edition, Volume 4
Harold F. Tipton and Micki Krause, Editors
ISBN: 0-8493-1518-2

Information Security Policies, Procedures, and Standards: Guidelines for Effective Information Security Management
Thomas R. Peltier
ISBN: 0-8493-1137-3

Information Security Risk Analysis
Thomas R. Peltier
ISBN: 0-8493-0880-1

Interpreting the CMMI: A Process Improvement Approach
Margaret Kulpa and Kurt Johnson
ISBN: 0-8493-1654-5

IS Management Handbook, 8th Edition
Carol V. Brown and Heikki Topi
ISBN: 0-8493-1595-6

Managing a Network Vulnerability Assessment
Thomas R. Peltier and Justin Peltier
ISBN: 0-8493-1270-1

A Practical Guide to Security Engineering and Information Assurance
Debra Herrmann
ISBN: 0-8493-1163-2

The Privacy Papers: Managing Technology and Consumers, Employee, and Legislative Action
Rebecca Herold
ISBN: 0-8493-1248-5

Securing and Controlling Cisco Routers
Peter T. Davis
ISBN: 0-8493-1290-6

Six Sigma Software Development
Christine B. Tayntor
ISBN: 0-8493-1193-4

Software Engineering Measurement
John Munson
ISBN: 0-8493-1502-6

A Technical Guide to IPSec Virtual Private Networks
James S. Tiller
ISBN: 0-8493-0876-3

Telecommunications Cost Management
Brian DiMarsico, Thomas Phelps IV, and William A. Yarberry, Jr.
ISBN: 0-8493-1101-2

AUERBACH PUBLICATIONS

www.auerbach-publications.com
To Order Call: 1-800-272-7737 • Fax: 1-800-374-3401
E-mail: orders@crcpress.com

STRATEGIC INFORMATION SECURITY

John Wylder

CRC Press
Taylor & Francis Group
Boca Raton London New York

CRC Press is an imprint of the
Taylor & Francis Group, an **informa** business

AN AUERBACH BOOK

CRC Press
Taylor & Francis Group
6000 Broken Sound Parkway NW, Suite 300
Boca Raton, FL 33487-2742

First issued in paperback 2019

© 2004 by Taylor & Francis Group, LLC
CRC Press is an imprint of Taylor & Francis Group, an Informa business

No claim to original U.S. Government works

ISBN-13: 978-0-8493-2041-5 (hbk)
ISBN-13: 978-0-367-39480-6 (pbk)
Library of Congress Card Number 2003059563

Library of Congress Cataloging-in-Publication Data

Wylder, John.
    Strategic information security / John Wylder.
      p. cm.
    Includes bibliographical references and index.
    ISBN 0-8493-2041-0 (alk. paper)
    1. Computer networks—Security measure. I. Title.

TK5105.59.W95 2003
005.8—dc22   2003059563

**Visit the Taylor & Francis Web site at
http://www.taylorandfrancis.com**

**and the CRC Press Web site at
http://www.crcpress.com**

Contents

Preface

This book represents a compilation of articles and ideas developed throughout my 14-year involvement in information security. When I first became the manager of a security department, the World Wide Web did not exist, viruses were infectious diseases humans caught, and networks were private and centralized. The Internet has since come to dominate discussions on security, and a host of new topics has been introduced that requires the attention of people involved in information security.

I have been fortunate to meet a number of experts in this field who have been kind enough to tolerate my sometimes slow learning curve, and I have developed a great respect for the pioneers in this field. People such as Chris Klaus with Internet Security Systems and Don Pipkin with Hewlett-Packard have been leading the way to help people protect their information and their computer systems. They and others like them serve as role models for those of us working in information security.

This book is my attempt at making a contribution to the field. My background includes years in application development and back office management and operations, so some of my ideas are based on this wide background prior to my security work. Along the way I have learned that a problem rarely has one solution and that every technical answer may have procedural and policy solutions as well.

I have written several articles about security. They form the basic framework of this book. Their general theme of linking management decision making with risk analysis led me to propose this book to Auerbach, and I was fortunate to have them agree to publish it.

The target audience for this book is the senior manager or executive in business who wants to learn more about information security. The goal is not to make everyone an expert after reading this book, but to help the reader understand the issues. It is my hope that by understanding these issues the reader will be better informed and make better decisions.

Security is really about teamwork. No person or group can expect to be successful working alone on something as complex as information security. Success requires the knowledge and effort of a team of people who are committed to a set of goals to be successful.

Security in a sense is a journey and not a destination. I hope you enjoy the ride.

Acknowledgments

I wish to thank a number of people for their assistance in the development of this book. First, I thank Rich O'Hanley and Auerbach for their continued interest in information security. I have been fortunate to work with Auerbach for over 11 years.

A number of people helped develop the material for this book. Ken Simone with Sungard Recovery Service and I have worked together for many years, and he has been a key person in educating me about business continuity planning. He also was kind enough to look at the chapter on that topic and make helpful comments that strengthened it.

James Lee and Phillip Stroud of Choicepoint were also very helpful. I talked to Phil about Choicepoint and he introduced me to Mr. Lee, who agreed to be interviewed. Choicepoint has a unique vision about information security, and both men serve as excellent spokesmen for that vision.

William Esterhuizen, CIO of a fortune 500 firm, is both a friend and a colleague. William is a great spokesman for information security and privacy, and serves as a role model. His grasp of this topic serves his company well, and his knowledge of security and privacy helped me to better understand some of the complex management issues that face a CIO.

Many other people whose names do not appear in the text have contributed greatly to my understanding of information security. They include Michael Howard and Angela Schwartz with Microsoft, and Chris Miller and Peter Penning with PricewaterhouseCoopers. All have been helpful and insightful. Their help in increasing my understanding is greatly appreciated.

I also want to thank colleagues who worked with me on security management issues through the years. Carlos Mena, CISO for Georgia Pacific, and Tony Samms, CISO for Norfolk Southern, are two of the best and I am indebted to them for their help and guidance through the years.

Last but not least I wish to mention my wife, Lyn Wylder. She also has been supportive of my efforts in writing this book, and her expertise in project management has helped me immensely.

JOHN WYLDER

Chapter 1
Introduction to Strategic Information Security

What Does It Mean to Be Strategic?

Recent events have led information security to gain greater importance as part of every business' risk management strategy. Most businesses today have at least a rudimentary security program in place, and many programs are evolving and growing in maturity. As these programs have grown, so has the need to move beyond the viewpoint that security is just a technical issue. Business is moving to a more mature position that security should be integrated into the very fabric of a business. In doing so, information security programs need to move from tactical implementations of technology to strategic partners in business.

What does it mean to say that security is "strategic?" How is this different than a strategy for an information security program? This book is aimed at answering these questions and will discuss major issues that affect both the security professional and the business person. There are other sources and material that address in greater depth the technical issues and solutions facing security professionals. Those books are important parts of their libraries and are complementary in nature to the information in this book. Rather than just repeat that material, this book also takes a fresh view of the information security world. These issues are viewed here primarily as a business problem and secondarily as a technical one. The goal is to bring together the interests of the business side of a company with those of the security professional and form a complete view of the problems as well as their potential solutions.

While there has been progress in information security, many companies today have not made the commitment to develop a complete information security program. Other companies have begun the process of creating security programs but have not integrated them into the rest of their businesses. Some businesses are trying to find the right reporting structure for security, looking at it as either an information technology function or a control function. All these issues point to an area that is still evolving when compared with more established roles such as auditing and finance. One of the other goals of this book is to educate the executive manager on the need to move his program along in its evolution and find ways to make it a core business function like those other areas.

Some companies, though, have taken an enlightened view of security. They believe that to be successful, they must demonstrate to their customers that security and the protection of information assets are core business functions. Those are companies with strategic information security programs.

One of those companies is Choicepoint, an Atlanta-based firm where information is the product. Choicepoint was created through spinning off a division of Equifax, the credit bureau company, in 1997. Choicepoint performs a variety of services (for example, employment verification) that make use of its extensive database of personal information. The mission statement of Choicepoint is one of the most comprehensive statements of the objectives of a sound information security strategy that can be found anywhere. The company's goal is "to be the most admired information company worldwide" by:

- Being the most valuable corporation in our industry
- Being one of the best places to work
- Being a demonstrated leader in social contribution
- Being a leader in the responsible use of information

Choicepoint builds on this theme in its vision statement:

> We strive to create a safer and more secure society through the responsible use of information.

The mission and vision show that, to Choicepoint, information protection is part of its corporate strategy and is not an added task. Securing information and protecting it is strategic to who Choicepoint is and what it does. At Choicepoint, according to James Lee, Chief Marketing Officer, this means security starts with embedding the ideals of information protection into the culture of the corporation. When an employee is hired, he is told from the start that information protection is his personal responsibility. Prior to their first day on the job new hires are given training in orientation classes on information security, and the culture of information protection is part of working at Choicepoint. Information security and protection is not something people do in addition to their work, it is their work.

Microsoft Corporation has long been a target in industry for failing to fully embrace the principles of information security and assurance. Many articles have been published that take Microsoft to task for failing in its duties to the public and its customers by not making security a priority. Recently, with its Trustworthy Computing Initiative, Microsoft has begun to send the message that they "get it" and security will now be part of its corporate culture. In a white paper on trustworthy computing, Microsoft defines this as follows:

> *Secure by design, secure by default, secure in deployment**

Bill Gates, chairman of Microsoft, wrote a memo addressing the issue of security. His letter appears on Microsoft's Web site (www.microsoft.com) and makes good reading for anyone interested in what it means to make security strategic. Many companies think that all it takes is a letter from the chairman for security to be claimed as a core value. Support from the executive office is where making security strategic starts, but in his letter Gates does more. He shows a road map for the journey it will take to make Microsoft products secure. His letter shows that as a business, Microsoft understands that this goal is important and that it cannot be achieved without the cooperation of everyone in the company.

While it remains to be seen how Microsoft will do in fulfilling this promise, the letters from Gates and their description of trustworthy computing are some of the best summations of what it means to have a strategic view of security. Security by design means that it is not an afterthought in the design process; instead, it is one of the requirements that designers use when starting a project. Secure by default means that a system comes with the security options turned on by default instead of set in the off position. Secure in deployment means that products will be shipped and ready to use in a way that will not compromise the security of the end user or other products. Those are big goals and worthy of any company wanting to achieve a world-class rating as a good business partner.

Not every company will have the same view of information that Choicepoint and Microsoft now have, but all companies can come to understand that information protection is critical to their success in today's world. Companies now work in a global, interconnected market and that makes the need to understand the power of information and the means to safeguard that information more important than ever.

The goal of protecting information and being a secure partner will not be one that can be achieved overnight. It will take a commitment of financial resources as well as a commitment of spirit. This starts with a thorough understanding of the problem and the risks a business faces. Once that level of understanding is achieved, then the correct steps can be taken to mitigate those risks. The final step in the journey is to measure the success

---

*Trustworthy Computing, Craig Mundie, Pierre de Vries, Peter Haynes, and Matt Corwine, Microsoft Corporation, October 2002.

of the security program and monitor it to ensure that it continues to function at the desired level. This book traces that effort and helps provide a road map for success.

Information Security Defined

In the broadest definition, an information security program is a plan to mitigate risks associated with the processing of information. The security profession has defined the basics of security as three elements:

1. *Confidentiality:* The prevention of unauthorized use or disclosure of information. Privacy is a closely related topic that has lately been getting more and more visibility.
2. *Integrity:* Ensuring that information is accurate, complete, and has not been modified by unauthorized users or processes.
3. *Availability:* Ensuring that users have timely and reliable access to their information assets.

These three elements — CIA — are the basics around which all security programs are developed. The three concepts are linked together in the idea of information protection. The idea that information is an asset that requires protection, just like any other asset of the business, is fundamental to understanding these concepts.

There has been a good deal of discussion among security professionals about updating this model and replacing the word "availability" with "authenticity." The idea behind these discussions is that availability is part of a separate discipline, business continuity planning, and that information security should stand alone as a distinct role. The security profession in general has stayed with the current definition. The concept of availability is a cornerstone of the profession to most people, as it addresses issues such as recovery from all types of incidents, not just disasters. Protecting information and information technology and making it available remains an accepted part of the security profession.

The Security Professional's View of Information Security

A broader view of what makes up the three elements of confidentiality, integrity, and availability can be found in looking at the ten domains of information security that make up the Common Body of Knowledge (CBK) maintained by the International Information Systems Security Certification Consortium (ISC²). The domains that make up the CBK further define the elements that make up CIA and help the business person and security professional understand the depth of the issues that guide the development of an effective information security program. The ten domains are:

1. *Access control systems and methodology:* These are the core application systems that people think of when discussing information security. This area addresses the use of information systems and how to manage and restrict access to a system or application.
2. *Telecommunications and network security:* This is similar to the first domain but addresses issues regarding transmission of information and the transport mechanisms regarding networks and connectivity.
3. *Security management practices:* This domain addresses policies and management practices, including risk management.
4. *Applications and systems development security:* This domain deals with the system development life cycle (SDLC) and data management from an information security perspective.
5. *Cryptography:* Covered in this domain are the principles and methods used to protect information through the use of codes and secrecy.
6. *Security architecture and models:* As the name indicates, this domain has to do with the design and architecture of computers and networks and how to protect them.
7. *Operations security:* This domain addresses the controls involved in the operation of a data center, and the management issues resulting from applications as they are used in a business environment.
8. *Business continuity planning (BCP) and disaster recovery planning (DRP):* This domain covers the policies and procedures needed to ensure that a business protects information resources from the effects of system failures and outages.
9. *Laws, investigations, and ethics:* This domain covers the legal and ethical issues for business.
10. *Physical security:* This domain covers the physical security measures that are involved in protecting the assets of the company.

Security as described by the information security profession takes on a decidedly technical look. Security professionals tend to be more comfortable looking at their problems from a highly technical perspective. For example, if a business wants to connect to the Internet to communicate using e-mail, the business person might assume that this is now a commonplace process that requires little thought to implement. The security professional, though, will want to discuss the e-mail system and any filtering rules on e-mail, and how the network itself is to be protected. If the company wants to move financial information across the same network, the security professional will bring up additional issues regarding the protection of confidentiality and the integrity of the message. The business person will tend to assume that the answers to these issues are simple and that they do not affect the business drivers, but the security professional believes that the opposite is true.

These two viewpoints can be a source of friction in a business. It is important to resolve these potential conflicts quickly and move forward with a joint view of the importance of securing information and developing a sound information security program. One approach to resolving the conflict of business security is to develop an information assurance program. In *Building a Global Information Assurance Program,** Curtis and Campbell describe in detail what this means and what it takes for a business to fully develop an effective information protection program. Their proposal is to have essentially a life cycle approach, instead of a more simple patchwork program that many technical people are comfortable pursuing.

The technical view of security focuses on solutions, product features, and implementation issues. Following are some of the questions asked by the security professional in this area:

Do we encrypt the message?
Do we use strong authentication or a simple user ID and PIN?
How should the network connect to outsiders? Should we build a separate network for the Internet, or should we connect our existing one using firewalls?

To the security professional these are important questions that require in-depth knowledge of the issues. The security professional wants to make the right decision because he understands the consequences of making the wrong one.

Most business people, though, are not as interested in how their information assets are protected. They want to ensure that the protection is cost-effective and takes into account business issues such as productivity and ease of use. The goals of the business person cannot be ignored, as he is the one who has to pay for security either in the form of product pricing or by explaining to a business partner that the added steps in a process are adding value to the product.

The Business View of Information Security

The CIA triad is one that most business managers can appreciate. With the recent explosive growth in privacy legislation, the confidentiality component gets a lot of interest today. Privacy to some business executives has become the core issue, sparking their interest in security information. In some cases this is reinforced by legislation and regulations such as the Health Insurance Portability and Accountability Act (HIPAA) and the Gramm–Leach–Bliley Act (GLBA). Those two acts have made accountability for protecting privacy a major issue for executives. These are not the only issues, though, facing the executive.

*Curtis, Raymond J. and Campbell, Douglas E., *Building a Global Information Assurance Program,* Auerbach Publications, New York, 2002.

The business executive adds in additional components to security, such as cost-effectiveness and ease of use, that often do not appear directly in the information security view of the problem. Risk to the business manager is not a binary "yes" or "no" process; it requires an understanding of the cost of protection, and a review of what alternatives exist and how to determine which is the best one to use. This is also a part of the evolution of the information security profession. Integrating the business view with the technical view is essential to moving security to a strategic role.

The business executive approaches issues such as those surrounding information security from the standpoint of risk management. Most executives are familiar with the principles of identifying risks, looking at risk mitigation strategies, and choosing the cost-effective approach to risk minimization. This is true whether we are talking about financial risks, investment risk, or product risk; in each case the business executive takes a standard approach to risk management. First comes an assessment phase. During this phase all relevant information is gathered regarding potential risks, outcomes, and probabilities of their occurrence. The next step is to prioritize those risks and address them by identifying the appropriate mitigation strategies. Sometimes the chosen strategy may involve further action steps; other times it may be appropriate to accept the risk as a normal course of business. Once the risks have been identified and the appropriate mitigation measures chosen, then business proceeds normally until there is an actual occurrence of that particular threat. At that point, the plans that have been developed are put into action and the problem is resolved.

In business, as stated earlier, this happens constantly. A business executive launches a new product looking at the financial implications, the revenue forecasts, and the prospects for competitive responses. Having done so, the next phase is execution. The product is launched and its success is measured. Plans are revised based on the response in the marketplace, and the cycle continues until something changes. With products involving information and information technology, the steps are the same.

It is therefore easy for the executive to understand the basic elements of risk management associated with information technology. The executive does not need a detailed understanding of the technology to be familiar with the concepts of risk assessment and risk mitigation; that is a normal part of the executive's job.

One thing that makes this subject different, though, is that many executives tend to delegate information technology risk to either the chief information officer (CIO), a lower-level manager in the information technology area, or an auditor. This seems similar to delegating the management of financial risks to the chief financial officer (CFO). What is different is that the CFO usually is a direct reporter to or even a peer of the CEO, but the CIO or the CIO's designee may be a level or two lower in the organization. That can create the impression that the risks associated with information technology are of less importance than those associated with the financial area of the company. Although that may have been true at one time, it has been changing recently. As shown through the vision statement at Choicepoint and the Trustworthy Computing Initiative at Microsoft, information technology and the risks associated with it are becoming integral parts of the business plans of most successful businesses today.

Changes Affecting Business and Risk Management

There are other events that have led the executive in business today to become increasingly more involved in issues that had formerly been the exclusive realm of the information security professional. This is an expanded view of the elements of the CIA triad. Confidentiality has given way to new laws and rules on privacy. Integrity has been expanded to include assurances of message authenticity and accuracy. Availability has been broadened to deal with threats from the Internet such as denial-of-service attacks and worms that slow down and impact e-mail and other forms of communication.

This evolution has also reached the political arena, as evidenced by the passage of privacy legislation such as:

- HIPAA: The Health Insurance Portability and Accountability Act, which covers privacy rules for people handling healthcare information.
- GLBA: The Gramm–Leach–Bliley Act, which describes privacy protection rules for the banking and financial services industry.
- COPA: The Children's Online Protection Act, which covers a broad area of information access and protection for children.

Each of these acts has added to the level of oversight that executives must apply to the information they use, process, or pass along. That has increased the sense of responsibility of the top executives and also put pressure on them to understand these issues and integrate their responses into their business culture.

The events of September 11, 2001, with the subsequent creation of the Department of Homeland Security, increased general awareness about security and information policies and protection. Firms that formerly were unconcerned about their roles in global communications now have learned that all businesses that process information face risks and threats from events outside of their industry and location. There are no safe locations or industries anymore; all businesses need to assess their roles in the global economy and how they need to prepare to deal with those risks.

Next followed the problems associated with the failures of major firms such as Enron that have led to revisions in policy coming from the Securities and Exchange Commission (SEC) and other regulatory agencies. Again, there is an added political dimension to these events, and the public outcry has resulted in the passage of the Sarbanes–Oxley Act. This legislation has placed a greater burden on executive management to prove that it is properly overseeing the actions of subordinates and making prudent decisions about its company. This law now requires that the executive signs off on the accuracy and integrity of financial statements. Integrity is one of the cornerstones of information security, and that makes Sarbanes–Oxley compliance an issue for the information security profession.

Good executives monitor the internal and external forces that affect their business plans. They understand that operating efficiency and execution may not be enough to survive if external events change the game they are playing. The combination of the events from September 11, 2001, and the financial breakdowns in accounting have significantly changed the focus for many executives.

The result of these external events has been both to increase the awareness of executive management of the issues driving information security and to place a greater burden on the managers to be involved in security management and oversight. This has been a mostly reactive approach to the problem rather than a planned or proactive one. The executives see the need to do something only in response to a direct threat, a new regulation, or revelations in the media. They have become involved in these decisions out of necessity, not out of a planned approach or as a value-add to their basic business.

The reactive approach may compound the problems that affect business. A proactive approach that makes security a part of the corporate strategy is a better choice. This means that policies have gone through the management review and approval process. Management can then point to existing policies, measure those against industry standards and regulatory guidance, and assess whether or not they have improved the situation. Failure to take a more aggressive approach can lead to embarrassing situations.

There are many decisions about risk reduction and security implementation that should be passed to the executive for review and approval. These decisions are part of the policy design and implementation process and require management to choose between several alternatives. The right choice will lead to reduced risk and improved control processes. The wrong choice can lead to problems. Some of the decisions that can have a major impact when looked at in the light of recent events are as follows:

- Record retention policies
- E-mail retention and deletion
- Opt-in or opt-out privacy statements
- Pornographic files on corporate servers
- Copyright issues and file sharing

Each day seems to bring another challenge that requires a response from management. There does not seem to be an end in sight to the increasing pressure on business to resolve these issues.

The business executive would likely rather spend his time dealing with customers or product issues. These executives do not want to learn a whole new discipline and a new set of technologies; instead, they want these problems resolved in a cost-effective manner, freeing them to move on to what are seen as more pressing issues. The problem for business is that the executive too often sees security issues as an additional burden to his or her already crowded agenda and not core to the business.

This is not true in all cases. Some firms that handle information on a daily basis make the protection of that information a core competency. These companies have seen the need to embed the principles of information security into everything they do. They have made the move from a reactive view of the problem to a strategic view.

Strategic Security

Some companies have embraced security as part of their business, but they may not have made it strategic. Even those companies that embrace the concept of security as a core business value may not appreciate the need to take it to an even higher level — that of making it strategic to the companies' business. This difference between being a core value and being strategic to the success of the company defines the major theme of this book.

It is not hard to find examples of the difference between a business merely saying that security is a core value and a business committing the resources and effort needed to make it part of the strategic plan of the company. Recently, the Georgia Institute of Technology announced that it had added a doctoral program in information security. This program will be added to the undergraduate school in information technology, which already had added an undergraduate degree in information security. In addition to degree-granting programs, the school has a business outreach program with courses in security offered as part of its continuing education effort. All of these programs indicate that the school had made a commitment to making information a core competency. Unfortunately, within a few weeks of that announcement, the school also announced that hackers had broken into a server at the school's arts center. The hackers had downloaded unprotected files containing private information including credit card data, names, and addresses. In announcing the break-in, the school said that the server in question lacked such basic protections as a firewall and intrusion-detection monitoring. What makes this interesting is that this school was announcing that it understood the importance of security but had not embraced it as part of its operational plans.

The risks involved in processing information or transacting business electronically are well known, and Georgia Tech should have been better prepared, especially in light of offering degree programs in information security. Why does this example not seem unusual? Why do businesses take on risk without the appropriate mitigation strategies in place? Part of the problem is a lack of understanding the extent of the problem. In the case of Georgia Tech, the school administration said that the server in question had not been included in its inventory of devices with external network access. The administration said that had it been aware of the server and the risks involved in using it, the school would have provided additional safeguards that might have prevented hackers from gaining access to the system.

Another key part of the problem that is cited repeatedly is a lack of commitment from the business executive. Security professionals routinely cite management commitment as one of the critical elements in developing a successful security program.

One of the first items that security professionals look for when starting a program is support from the executive team. Almost all books and articles that describe effective security programs start with the need to have senior management support, which often takes the form of a letter from the CEO embracing the goals of the information security program. The letter is in a standard format and often looks as shown in Exhibit 1.

This type of support is important but it does not guarantee the success of the information security program. Managers still have to buy into the details of the program and embrace it in their day-to-day activities. Having a letter from the CEO is good; having the CEO be part of the solution is better.

The letter from Bill Gates at Microsoft serves as an example. If Microsoft had stopped with just a letter from the chairman, then nothing would be expected to have really changed. Having the chairman lead the project and announce that he was personally making it a core business value is very different, and it will ensure that the necessary changes actually take place.

Moving to a view that security is strategic requires a different mindset. It requires a view that all phases of the business will integrate security as part of their daily work and will include security in their operational activities. This is a major shift that requires the support of the executive office.

Exhibit 1. Letter to Employees

To: All Employees, XYZ Corporation

From: CEO

To my fellow employees,

I am announcing today the start of a new program aimed at protecting one of our most important assets, our information. For this program to be successful, everyone — from me on down — will be involved in this effort.

The effort will be led by Ms. S. Smith, Director of Information Security, who will be setting up a series of meetings to announce the details. She has my full cooperation and support.

Please join me in supporting her efforts as we move forward in our business plans.

John Doe
CEO

That support will be called on again and again, especially when it comes time to pay for the additional tools and features that are needed as part of the implementation process.

There is also a difference between security strategy and strategic security. This book discusses elements of the strategy involved in developing an effective information security program. Those elements include all of the ten domains of the CBK. Strategy is about people, policies, and procedures. Strategic security, though, is about involving those elements in every facet of the corporation and doing so in a way that makes it part of everyone's job and not something that will be added later.

The story of Microsoft and its change in approach to security needs to be discussed in detail to emphasize how important that change is to the company, its customers, and the information technology industry as a whole. Microsoft has long been a company that has had to battle the impression that security is not strategic to its business. For years, security professionals complained about the fact that Microsoft seemed to see security as something that was done after the fact and not part of its daily business. Some of the complaints were that Microsoft products came with the security settings turned off, making it the responsibility of the customer to turn them on. Other complaints included perceived failures to test features and functions for security prior to releasing them to customers, again placing the burden of security on the customer side of the equation. This led to a lot of frustration by customers with complaints that Microsoft did not understand its role in secure computing.

This changed when Microsoft announced the creation of a new initiative, Trustworthy Computing. In his announcement, Bill Gates indicated that Microsoft was going to move beyond looking at security as an added activity and instead would embrace it as strategic to the business. He said that he knew this would be difficult as it would mean a cultural shift in the way Microsoft does business. That is what it means to take security from tactical to strategic. Microsoft has done more than just print a letter from Bill Gates announcing its commitment to the principles of secure computing. At Microsoft today, security issues are being embedded into product development discussions. Although adding features that benefit the customer is still the first goal of the company, those features must be weighed against the need to do so in a safe and secure manner.

According to a statement from a Microsoft corporate white paper, available at www.microsoft.com, the following are the goals that any trustworthy computing has to set:

- *Goals:* The basis for a customer's decision to trust a system.
- *Security:* The customer can expect that systems are resilient to attack, and that the confidentiality, integrity, and availability of the system and its data are protected.
- *Privacy:* The customer is able to control data about himself, and those using such data adhere to fair information principles.
- *Reliability:* The customer can depend on the product to fulfill its functions when required to do so.
- *Business integrity:* The vendor of a product behaves in a responsive and responsible manner.

This makes a good list for other companies to begin with as they devise their own approaches to the definition of strategic security. In making the transition to a strategic view of security, each company must examine a similar list of values and select those that affect its particular business line. Having done so, each company can then move on to the incorporation of those values into its operations.

A generalized list of the strategic role of information security may be based on the following core values:

- Information is an asset that is critical to the success of the business. As a result, the information assets of the company must be protected against relevant risks.
- Information security must be integrated with business plans.
- Customers should expect that the company will respect their privacy and protect their information with the same diligence that will be used to protect its own information.

The latter is a variation of the Golden Rule: treat others as you want to be treated.

Making the transition to a strategic view of security will also involve measuring the execution against those values. It is easier to speak of a commitment to secure computing than it is to actually do the things necessary to bring that about. There also has to be a shift in the strategy involved in the implementation of security policy and procedures. The letter from the CEO starts the process, but that is not where it will end.

Strategic Security or Security Strategy?

There is a difference between creating a strategy for information security and having a strategic view of information security. A strategy for information security is important even if information security has not been elevated to a strategic role in a business.

A good definition of what is meant by a strategy for security can be found in the Information Security Booklet from the Federal Financial Institutions Examination Council (FFIEC) Information Technology Examination Handbook. In it, there is a chapter dedicated to defining and describing a strategy for security and how it can be measured to determine whether or not it will be successful. This section of the handbook starts with the definition of an information security strategy as "a plan to mitigate risks while complying with legal, statutory, contractual, and internally developed requirements." The FFIEC further describes the strategy to include:

- Cost comparisons of different strategic approaches to the institution's environment and complexity.
- Layered controls that establish multiple control points between threats and organization assets.
- Policies that guide officers and employees in implementing the security program.

This approach speaks to security as a control function and the need to have a plan that covers all aspects of that function. It also points out that there will be a layered approach based on different threats and risks to the business. This shows the need to develop a good planning process and a strategy to implement that process for all the diverse functions within the bank. What this statement does not do is address the issue of making security a strategic function, one that would co-exist equally with other critical business operations.

This approach, however, does lead to ways to identify what it means to say an information security program is strategic to a business. The FFIEC, for example, in that same handbook recommends checking to see if there are standards in place at the board of directors level guiding the security strategy that management has chosen. The handbook recommends that the auditor look to see if:

- The board or an appropriate committee approves each of the electronic systems based on a written strategic plan and risk analysis commensurate with the activity.
- The board establishes appropriate standards and procedures for overall program administration and systems operation.
- Management provides adequate training and retraining of officers and employees on proper controls and potential risks associated with alternative delivery and payment systems.
- Information is secure and the bank's internal system(s) is (are) adequately protected against attacks from both internal and external sources.*

Although banking as a regulated industry tends to lead the field when it comes to identifying risks and assigning responsibilities, these standards are ones that could apply to any business in any industry. By identifying the board of directors as the ones responsible for ensuring that appropriate policies and procedures are in place, understood by employees and management, and appropriately enforced, the FFIEC places information security as a strategic issue on a par with any other form of risk management.

Monitoring and Measurement

Along with changing the view of security to a strategic one and then creating the appropriate strategy, it is also necessary to measure progress and monitor the success of the program. It is not sufficient to publish a list of policies and announce management's support for those policies; there must be a process for management to use to validate the appropriateness of and compliance with written policies. If the policies exist only on paper, security of the company will not have been advanced at all.

There must also be put in place a way to maintain those rules and update them as conditions change. Those changes must be tested and the implementation process has to be documented and integrated with the other change management procedures that are in place. The threats and risks to business today are constantly changing and require a flexible response, one that takes into account the ongoing business on the one hand, and the need to constantly address threats and risks on the other hand.

Another strategic challenge for management is how to organize a response to security management. Security information, even when it is

---

*Federal Financial Institutions Examination Council (FFIEC) Information Technology Examination Handbook, June 1998, available at www.ffiec.gov.

compartmentalized into one area, involves sifting through large amounts of information in real-time. In a complex organization, there are alerts from firewalls, intrusion-detection systems, audit trails, and messages from operating systems, all of which need to be analyzed and evaluated before an appropriate response can be formulated. In many organizations, this has led to the institution of a Computer Security Incident Response Team (CSIRT) (see Chapter 11). Other organizations have outsourced the monitoring of key elements of their security infrastructure and let outside agencies handle the first-response duties. Whichever strategy is chosen, there needs to be policies and procedures in place to handle incidents when they occur and there needs to be an escalation plan to notify management appropriately. These options will be explored in detail in later chapters.

Moving Forward

This book is all about making information security strategic to the business. Information security is a rapidly evolving field that is becoming more and more important to the success of all businesses, large or small. Familiarizing executives with security is part of this effort.

In the chapters that follow, the role of security is examined in detail and solutions are proposed to embed security practices and principles into the business. Some of this is as technical as is necessary to explain how the controls will function, to build a case for the need for having those controls in place. Other parts of this discussion center on how to manage the security role within the context of general business management, treating it in the same way as other management control functions. Looking at security as more than a technical issue will help both the security practitioner and the business person look at their respective roles in their company and find ways to work better together on common goals.

This book also offers a blueprint for a discussion that needs to take place at every company and business that uses computers or accesses networks. This discussion covers basic corporate governance issues as well as the roles and responsibilities for management and staff. Although the discussion may vary depending on the type of business and the risk profile of the industry, it is one that needs to take place for a company to succeed in its business goals and fiduciary responsibilities. No matter how different one business or industry thinks it is from others, this discussion needs to take place and should not be put off to the future. Each business executive needs to understand these issues and also understand what the choices are to address the risks they face. Once a company has examined the role of security and made the assessment of how to incorporate it into the business, it will have developed a strategic view that will help that company to minimize risk and protect key assets. Those are basic functions of all business that cannot be ignored.

Section I
Organizational Issues

This section covers a wide variety of issues that affect the organizational structure of a business with respect to information security. There are many choices that face the executive management team as it confronts the risk of doing business in today's highly computerized and interconnected economy. It is no longer practical to ignore the risks that come with having a Web presence or using e-mail. In the past, it might have been possible to delegate those issues to a technical person far down on the organizational chart. Today, those issues require the understanding and commitment of the CEO and the CFO to be dealt with successfully.

Chapter 2
The Life Cycles
of Security Managers

Introduction

The evolution of data processing from mainframes to distributed processing to the Internet has resulted in many changes. Businesses have changed the way they process their data and the way they view the people who manage that process. In the beginning, there was the data center manager (typically an operations job in middle management), then the director of computing services, and finally the chief information officer. The evolution of these various management positions is indicative of changes that have occurred throughout the entire organization, and in few areas has that been more obvious than in the way organizations view data (now often referred to as information) security.

In organizations today, distributed processing has changed the way the information is viewed as well as the way it is managed. Centralization is no longer the preferred means of departmental organization, and distributed information processing has gained increased popularity, causing significant changes in business. These changes continue to occur, just as jobs for the rest of the information systems industry continue to evolve.

Departmental roles also continue to be redefined. The relationship of such groups as auditors to the people responsible for managing information (e.g., the information security manager and the information systems manager) is also changing. Partnerships are becoming more important as the roles of auditors and security become interdependent.

In the area of information security, these changes have necessitated a thorough reexamination of the skills needed to perform that function. It is no longer enough to attempt to protect the information on one system or network; now it is necessary to manage the protection of a diverse group of business information assets spread throughout the organization.

The Information Security Manager's Responsibilities

The duties of the information security manager are typically focused on two distinct functions: authentication and authorization. In authentication, the security manager's task is to identify the user or service requesting access to a particular system or information resource. This is simply the "who are you" aspect of security, and it is the most commonly understood aspect because it deals with user IDs and passwords. The user ID can be known to many employees, but the password should be known only to its user. The password is the actual element that performs the authentication of the user.

Authorization deals with a more complex concept: privilege. Users may be given access to a computer system or a resource, but what they can do with that resource is defined as their privilege or authority. After users are properly authenticated, their privileges are verified so that they can perform their duties. In terms that auditors favor, this is a complicated equation of balancing need-to-know against risk to the organization. Most users have a want-to-know that exceeds their need-to-know, and the information security manager has to balance the needs and wants against the risks and threats to the organization.

The tasks of authentication and authorization are easier in a small company than in a large one. A small company may have limited amounts of information or data that it handles, and although the structure of the data may be complex, the lack of volume makes the task of balancing risks and privileges easier. Usually, the data is centralized, whether it is in the mind of the owner of the organization or in a microcomputer, making the information easy to obtain. In a large organization, the tasks are made more complicated by larger databases and structures and by the flow of information throughout the organization from distributed processing. It is this evolution from simple data structures to complex information flow that is the challenge for the managers of both the processing and protection of information. This is both a technical and a personnel problem affecting the relationships of the business components of the organization as well as the relationship of the data elements.

The Evolution of Data Security to Information Security

In a small company with a single owner and only a few employees, the data processing jobs are all performed centrally and all information flow can easily be controlled. There is typically a single point of contact for the decisions surrounding authentication and authorization. The person responsible for making these decisions, often the organization's owner (or president), is therefore the *de facto* security manager.

When the organization grows, the users of computer-based information move into smaller and more diverse units. Decisions about access and authentication involve more people and become increasingly complex to administer and control. Important questions about the need to know arise, and the answers can be ambiguous because there are more users making the requests for access to information they need to know and more locations where the information can reside.

The degree of privilege becomes an issue: does the person need only to be able to read the information or to be able to change it as well? Identifying just who is (or should be) authorized to make such decisions often becomes as difficult as making the decisions.

The final phase of this evolution occurs when the data itself becomes decentralized throughout the organization. Then the issues of authentication and authorization become extremely difficult for the information security manager to resolve; this is the situation that exists in most businesses today.

The effect of decentralization on the securing of corporate information assets is to force a change in viewpoint. The job of security, once regarded as a matter of data security, is now considered one of information security, as the sum of the data elements is worth more than the individual parts. Databases now feed information to midrange machines and personal computers where there is additional processing performed.

The job of the data security manager broadens to encompass all the data elements as they flow through the organization. Just as the raw materials are assembled to make a finished product, so must the data elements be assembled into information. The task is then to secure all the data throughout that production life cycle.

The Repository Concept

One well-documented example of a means for securing data throughout the life cycle was the concept of the repository from IBM and its related Systems Application Architecture (SAA). Here the emphasis is on the use of a variety of processor platforms, all working with information that is housed first on a large centralized database. That data is then downloaded throughout the organization to the other processors for updating and analysis. Later, the process is reversed as information is updated for storage on the large database. In this way, IBM hoped to maximize the capabilities of each type of processor, while minimizing storage cost.

The more recently developed single sign-on systems using a Lightweight Directory Access Protocol (LDAP) directory are similar to this concept. User authentication rules are kept in a single database and users only sign on once; their credentials are verified and they are then authorized to access all systems to which they have rights. This is a complex process as the user enrollment process must include all systems that any user may need within the network. Maintaining the linkage between all those systems requires complex planning and sound managerial processes.

This repository concept inevitably leads to many changes in the way the flow of information is managed and, in particular, in the responsibility for the processing of the information. Whereas the data center manager once provided the data security manager with a single-point-of-contact, along with distribution of data, there is now a distribution of responsibilities.

Most organizations now have distributed IT management information centers and to end-user computing functions. The traditional data center managers share the various responsibilities for information processing. Roles are clearly defined in this shared environment. Usually, the data center manager controls the large CPU, and the IC manager may only offer advice and guidance on the use of certain hardware and software. Individual departments and divisions may also be held responsible for their local processors and data. This has caused the security manager to have to shift from a single-point-of-contact to multiple-points-of-contact to cover security issues, requiring new and different skills.

Changing Job Requirements

Distributed processing has also had a direct effect on the choice of the person responsible for information security. Where security was once viewed as a technical issue and handled solely on a mainframe in which all the data assets resided, security is now viewed as a process that must match the flow of information throughout the organization. This information must be examined from all the differing viewpoints of users, operators, and security to balance the need to access the information against the need to protect it.

The security manager now has to secure the information itself as well as the flow of that information, not just static data. The entire process now requires a different set of skills than was formerly required for the task of simple data security. These skills have evolved from the purely technical to encompass business skills as well. The position has evolved away from one that is tied with the information technology area to one that has more global responsibilities with closer ties to the business areas.

Business Life Cycles and the Evolution of an Information Security Program

A common way to understand products is to view them in the context of a product life cycle. The conventional life cycle curve featuring an introductory phase, a growth phase, and a maturity phase can be used to understand both products and processes. Products move along this curve, going from the introductory phase, in which they penetrate a small part of a market, to the maturity phase, in which market share is maximized.

This life cycle can be applied to information security by overlaying processors (mainframes, midrange computers, servers, and personal computers) and their related information security products on the life cycle curve. To do this, substitute on the y-axis either the percentage of information assets handled by each type of processor or their relative importance to the business for market share. Then, through use of conventional wisdom, the state of security on mainframes, midrange computers, and microcomputers can be graphically illustrated.

Mainframes and their security systems, which have been around for years in the guise of such products as Computer Associates' ACF-2 and IBM's RACF, would be placed in the maturity phase of the life cycle. Midrange computers would appear in the latter growth stage. These machines started out filling a variety of needs, mostly as single-purpose processors, a role that today is usually filled by servers and personal computers. In some cases, midrange machines were actually the organization's mainframes, but this was not the most usual application. Midrange systems have been giving way to servers over the last several years, and it may be appropriate to think of the two terms as synonymous today. Servers have been in place long enough that they are in the latter growth stage now, moving into the maturity stage.

Despite the longevity of computers, new processor architectures keep arriving, and their security systems are often less well developed. This resurgence of midrange machines, especially in the role of fault-tolerant processors, places them in the growth stage rather than in the maturity stage as their product age might otherwise dictate. Microcomputers were an even newer product with security systems that were much less developed. In 1989, Computer Associates introduced its first microcomputer-based security package, and IBM added significant controls, first to its AS400 line and then in the TIVOLI systems management product and now has filled out its security product line. Other manufacturers have kept pace with their own products.

The purpose of a graphical view is to illustrate the relative state of security products on the various computer platforms. Mainframe security is generally well established and understood by both the security manager and the business manager. Security for microcomputers is a much newer field, and the products and requirements for this type of security are less well defined. Internet security is also in the early growth phase in this view.

The varying levels of product maturity have a similar effect on the manager responsible for securing information in the business. As data center managers have with the products and platforms they use, most security managers have more experience with mainframe security than with microcomputer security. For example, the Office of the Comptroller of the

Currency, the oversight group for information processing in the banking world, issued its first set of guidelines for distributed systems in 1989. Therefore, like the processors they run on, both the products and even the specification for distributed systems are in the introductory phase of the life cycle.

The following sections examine each of the life cycle phases — introductory, early growth, rapid growth, and maturity — as they pertain to the security manager's roles and responsibilities. This way, the evolution from data processing to business information flow in the organization can be matched with the evolutionary changes in the responsibilities and skills of the security manager.

The Introductory Phase

When an information security program is introduced into an organization, the security manager's first task is to obtain senior management support. This is an important step because it establishes an emphasis on the proper concern: the corporate view of information. After obtaining senior management support, the security manager identifies the tasks associated with the authentication of users and their authorization to access data.

Typically, the first security manager is a technician, experienced in the particular operating system of the central processor in use, and is often given security as an additional duty. The primary job of these managers may remain that of systems programmers, with responsibility for operating system functions. They generally do not possess management or administration skills, which are superfluous at this point, as the use of automation is seen as a technical rather than a business issue. They may have certifications in the products they support and may be experts in the technologies, but security is just another task added to their daily job.

As in the simple business structure described earlier, the data being processed during the introductory phase is centralized, and the person assigned to that role has the appropriate skill level. The security program is designed around the concept of a central database with limited points of contact and hierarchical rule structures based on centralized management. The security of data during this phase is seen more as a technical issue than as a management issue. This applies whether or not the processor is an actual mainframe or a smaller unit.

The Early Growth Phase

In this phase, the number of users on the mainframe begins to grow, and the demands on the skills of the security manager begin to increase. Instead of being limited to dealing with purely technical tasks, the security manager must write policies and develop procedures to handle the growing user population. Any distributed processing is typically of a stand-alone nature (i.e., not connected to an enterprise communications network).

The demands on the security function increase with the growing workload, and at this point the job is often made a full-time position for the first time. The original manager of the security function, a technician, often gives way to an administrative security manager who may have fewer technical skills but greater organizational skills, consistent with the changes in the needs of the job. Technical issues may then be referred back to the previous security manager or to a technical support area. Security policies are much more formalized at this point, calling on a greater need for administrative expertise.

As the mainframe and central database user population increases and requires greater administrative skills from the security manager, growth in distributed processing also occurs. The change in the number and types of processors that need security calls for a variety of new technical skills. These processors and systems could be called divisional (i.e., stand-alone processors or networks managed remotely) because they address specific business functions and often do not have a link to the mainframe. The network itself is a control point for access to information and applications.

Some centralized security managers may not even be aware that these distributed processors exist because they may be purchased and installed remotely. And even if the security managers are aware, they may develop a set of simple rules by ascribing a low risk to these processors and the information they store. Risk assessment is usually done informally during this phase, and the central database is generally viewed as the repository for the most valuable data assets of the organization.

This process can be hampered by the fact that the security managers are often unskilled in processors and security systems other than those that run on the mainframe (or another primary processor). Without the knowledge of the technology of different systems, the security manager is in a poor position to judge the requirements for security.

In addition, managing in a distributed systems environment requires greater interpersonal and organizational skills. These systems, if purchased and managed separately, are difficult to control in a centrally managed security process.

The Rapid Growth Phase

In this phase, the use of data processing extends deeper into every facet of the business; in fact, it becomes essential to most jobs. In addition, the use of stand-alone processors and microcomputers becomes widespread, and these systems are interfaced to the larger processor. The number of users continues to grow, placing increased demands on the administrative skills of the security manager.

It is also during this phase of the security manager life cycle that the skill requirements begin to change, and frequently a different person is chosen for the position. Where the predecessors were skilled technicians or low-level administrators, the growth of distributed processing and the concomitant use of a variety of processors and platforms creates a demand for a manager with a different set of skills.

The emphasis now is on organizational and procedural issues across process and division lines. Frequently, the person chosen comes from a back-office function such as personnel or finance, as those areas are usually familiar with administration across the entire organization. This is not the same as managing the flow of the information throughout the organization; the focus is on the discrete rules that are being developed for each different use of information. This security manager frequently places the emphasis on centralization and control, essentially using a bureaucratic approach. Policies become the focal point of the manager's activities and there is a strong preference for solving any security issue first through the creation of a new policy rather than a technical solution.

Exhibit 1 shows the different skill sets for security managers.

Exhibit 1. Security Manager Skill Chart: Security Managers' Skill Set for Different Environments

Skills Required	Data Location	Complexity of Database	Reliance on Data
Technical	Centralized	Simple	Low
Administrative	Centralized	Simple	Medium
Bureaucratic	Limited decentralization	Medium	Medium to high
Technocratic	Decentralized	High	High

The skills that are of low importance at this point are often the technical skills that were emphasized so strongly in the first security manager's background. Security is seen as a requirement independent of technology, one that can be managed through the efficient administration of corporate policies and procedures.

The Maturity Phase

In the maturity phase, distributed technology is fully developed within the organization. The power of the independent processors and their value to the users puts the greatest strain on the attempts to control security from a centralized location point. The Internet and wireless technology have increased the strain on centralized management. End users can add wireless networks without authorization; marketing managers may add Web sites for special projects that bear the company logo but are not directly attached to the corporate network. These are real challenges to the skill of the security manager.

In most organizations, users are now responsible for their own data and their own passwords.* Previously, users were seen as responsible only for their passwords or the authentication aspect of security. In the context of distributed processing, however, users are now responsible for the authorization aspect as well.

In a broader sense, distributed processing gives end users control over their data processing requirements and it makes them responsible for protecting and securing their own data. The skills needed to manage information security in their environment are quite different from those required when the data is centralized.

These new skills for the security manager include the following classes (as shown in Exhibit 1):

- *Technical:* This class requires thorough knowledge of operations systems, systems software, and networks, and limited knowledge of business functions and procedures. These are typically the skills of a systems programmer.
- *Administrative:* This class requires mid-level knowledge of technology and technical issues, and understanding of rules, procedures, and processes. Little supervisory knowledge or experience is required; emphasis is on clerical skills.
- *Bureaucratic:* This class requires novice-level knowledge of technology and a background that emphasizes organizational skills and development of rules and procedures. Problems are first seen as procedural rather than technical.
- *Technocratic:* This class requires strong technical training and experience, but may be at a higher level than operating systems (e.g., those required for an applications programmer or systems analyst). Managerial experience in a variety of groups as well as general business knowledge and experience are necessary.

Some of the new skills needed are technical, as processors are often linked together in wide area networks (WANs) or local area networks (LANs), and the various processors have different capabilities for handling the required security. There is also a need for greater personnel skills, as the rules for security developed for this phase must emphasize local accountability instead of centralized administration. This emphasizes the

---

*J. Von Kadich, keynote address at the Computer Security Institute Conference, Atlanta, Georgia, 1990.

need for managers to bring various departments together under a common understanding, rather than simply issuing rules and policies.

Just as the mainframe today is located in the maturity phase (or even in the decline), the role of the security manager in a widely distributed data environment may also be located in that phase. The technical and administrative skills needed are more clearly defined, and the responsibilities are broader and more fully developed. This could be called the technocratic approach to security.

This approach can lead to some conflicts with other managers. For example, the manager of the end user systems-support function may believe that some of the responsibility for securing servers, personal computers, and LANs is exclusively his or should at least be shared. Likewise, the network manager may feel that remote access is part of his job functions and may be reluctant to give someone else that authority. This is similar to the problems encountered in the introductory phase: the data center manager might object to security procedures if they interfere with the ability to process jobs and meet schedules and deadlines. The resolution of conflicts such as these requires a corporatewide view of the security function.

Skill Changes over Time

The type of person chosen to fill the role of security manager may change depending on where in the life cycle an organization falls. In the early phases, a limited-function position emphasizing technical and administrative skills may be appropriate.

Later, it may be necessary to redefine the job to bring other skills into play. The introduction of distributed processing and the resulting demands for greater user autonomy along with the divergent technologies will eventually put the greatest demands on the person chosen for the security manager's role.

It is also possible to view the different skills needed by the security manager by charting the complexity of the processing, the diversity of data locations, and the reliance on the information in the organization. The introduction of the concept of complexity is to allow for the use of large scientific databases that have a basically simple structure. This contrasts with the customer database used in a trust department that contains everything from investments to names and addresses. Both of these may be large files, but one has a much more complex structure than the other.

Conclusion

Another change may also be occurring that emphasizes the new skill requirements for the security manager. The roles and relationships of auditors and security professionals are also evolving. Traditionally, the auditing function is seen as a separate business function, independent, isolated, and responsible for testing the strength of existing business controls.

In this distributed computing environment, the security manager should work more closely with the auditors to ensure the quality and the efficiency of the controls needed. The ability to work alone using the auditor as a final checkpoint is deemphasized, as the technology is changing too fast to allow the functions to operate totally independently. The impartial review that an audit staff offers is still needed, but there also needs to be greater teamwork between the audit staff and the security manager. Auditors can act in an advisory role and still not compromise their independence.

The person chosen to manage the information security function in a complex organization may have a diverse background featuring in-depth technical, managerial, and administrative skills. All these skills are required when the information becomes distributed throughout the entire organization, and it is the flow of this information as well as the information itself that needs to be secured. Through these diverse skills, the security manager can maintain both the needed level of security as well as have an effective method for implementation of the security policies consistent with the business needs of the organization.

Chapter 3
Chief Security Officer or Chief Information Security Officer

Introduction

The idea of elevating operational roles to be peers of business executives is a relatively recent phenomenon. This is the realm of what are now called C-level managers, which started with the creation of the Chief Information Officer (CIO) position and later led to the creation of a number of related positions: Chief Technology Officer (CTO), Chief Privacy Officer (CPO), Chief Information Security Officer (CISO), and Chief Security Officer (CSO). Together these have gotten their own grouping and are jointly referred to with their business peers, the Chief Financial Officer (CFO) and Chief Executive Officer (CEO) as the C-level positions in an organization. The idea of creating peer titles and roles for the technical managers was to emphasize the importance of those jobs within an organization and to also give them enough power and authority to be effective.

These roles have not been universally accepted in business. There are many companies that do not yet have a C-level role for the information technology team. Those companies are content to stay with a more traditional organizational structure. That type of organization is usually built around a split of operational and revenue-generating responsibilities. The operational side of the business has the information technology areas (computer operations, networks, help desk) and any other significant back-office functions. The other side of the company is usually organized along either geographic or business lines. This type of structure does not lend itself to the C-level titles, and the managers are listed as either Director of Operations or Vice President of Operations. The security role in those organizations may report to either the Vice President of Information Technology or the equivalent. This has not changed in business over the last 20 years.

The security and privacy positions, however, have received a great deal of attention since September 11, 2001, with the passage of privacy legislation (the Health Insurance Portability and Accountability Act (HIPAA), the Children's Online Protection Act (COPA), the Gramm–Leach–Bliley Act (GLBA), and their European equivalents) as well as the most recent events leading to the creation of the Department of Homeland Security in the United States. These events have challenged the traditional organizational structures in business. Establishing the roles of management and the organizational structure is the responsibility of the executive management team. It is up to the CEO, the CFO, and the President to establish the structure below them and ensure that it properly reflects their goals and the mission of the company. The decision to establish other C-level positions is one that should be reviewed at length and made in light of the importance of technology and technology controls to that organization.

Deciding on the importance of security and privacy to the executive team is a more complex issue. It is one thing to sign off on a pledge to maintain the privacy and integrity of information; it is something else entirely to give the people managing that function a seat at the table. Should security be a peer with the business team? Is privacy as important as the business line chief or the head of production services? This chapter explores the role of security in management and looks at the alternative approaches to placing that role at the "C" level. This will involve an in-depth review of the responsibilities for managing security and what the choices are for placing those responsibilities in the organization.

Organizational Issues

When it comes to looking at the role of information security in an organization, looking at historical precedents does not provide much guidance. Just as the idea of establishing technology management as a peer to business management is still controversial today, so is the idea of making security a separate box on the organization chart. Other areas, such as procurement or work safety, may also be important to a business, and elevating one to a higher level is a value-based decision that can have repercussions.

One reason that security is not always viewed highly is that for many companies it has been justified using fear as the driving issue. Fear of hackers, viruses, service interruptions, information theft, and industrial espionage has all been part of the way security has been justified to management. The related justification is the idea of using actual events to drive future plans. Any organization that has already experienced one or more of these problems is automatically seen as more receptive to increasing the role and visibility of security. The idea is that someone who has felt the pain from an absence of security is someone who will understand the benefits of preventive actions.

The alternative is to find positive benefits to the role of security in business. This means looking for ways that securing information may be perceived by the customer as an added value, something that will make him willingly pay more for goods or services. That means trying to find a return on the investment a business makes in security.

Justifying the Importance and Role of Security in Business

Trying to develop a return on investment (ROI) for security has been one of the goals of consultants, vendors, and security professionals for many years. This has been seen as desirable as it moves away from the fear-and-pain approach to a more proactive, business-minded one.

This process of establishing a security ROI begins with gathering all the cost data. The costs of security are generally either well known or easy to document; the problem is finding a way to document the benefits of security. A list of security costs includes items that most people in information technology are familiar with:

- Security software and hardware, including authentication systems, firewalls, intrusion-detection systems, and anti-virus applications
- Operational costs, including help desks, employee ID enrollment, and maintenance of access credentials
- Storage costs
- Training and education
- Remote access systems
- Audit systems and audit reporting

Each of these items has costs that are easy to identify and quantify. Software cost is easy to document, as is the cost of remote access controls such as virtual private networks (VPNs) of other technologies. Audit systems add to this list and include their own overhead as audit logs must be maintained and preserved, increasing system storage requirements. There are other storage and network capacity costs that have to be added to this list with the increased usage of the Internet. For example, employees using high-speed corporate networks have the means today to download and store music files, photographs, and even digital movies on corporate servers and storage areas. Although the effects of such actions are an operational- and even a legal-liability issue, the controls of these actions usually fall into the lap of the information security manager as it is similar to other duties already on his list.

Related directly to these costs are the time spent by employees signing onto systems, the cost of maintaining passwords, e-mail controls, and content filters. The latter are some of the latest additions in the security manager's arsenal and have become routine in most businesses. Firms today understand that they have responsibility to ensure the productivity of their staff and also to protect themselves from the liabilities that may be associated with employees accessing controversial Internet sites or using company systems and networks for personal business. Along with the storage issues, downloading of music and movies exposes a company to copyright liability. These actions may be hard to quantify as a cost, but it remains an issue with potential for financial liability if it does occur and is discovered by an outside agency. At the least, there can be an estimate of the potential liability from a lawsuit arising from this activity.

While these costs exist, even the easily quantifiable ones may not be sufficient to make the case for increased budgets for security, let alone increasing the visibility of the role of security management. That leads to the necessity of finding items on the other side of the ledger, the benefit side. This has proven to be much more difficult to industry professionals than it would first appear. A recent search on the Internet using the terms "ROI" and "information security" turned up over 473,000 entries, not one of which was a tool accepted by industry to help with this calculation. So despite all that material, no consensus exists to guide managers through this exercise.

That leads the analyst back to looking at the list of costs and trying to find related items that can be included in the calculations. In some cases the benefit may be reduced cost or cost avoidance. For example, having a good security program may protect against the possibility of regulatory fines. There are other items that may make the list using this expanded view of costs and benefits. Some of the elements that would help define this argument include the following:

- Cost of financial losses from a security breach
- Regulatory penalties
- Reduced overhead from simplifying access controls
- Reduced costs from password synchronization and employee enrollment activities

Note that this list of benefits is almost exclusively a list of cost avoidance. Some security professionals have even coined terms to explain this, such as CINI (cost of no investment) or ROSI (return on security investment). Changing the name does not make it a benefit, however; it merely points out one of the realities of security — that it is a cost of doing business. Security then can be viewed as a cost that brings with it overhead and additional layers of systems and business management.

That is not to say that not having security is a viable option. In most cases, not having security will lead to real expenses that in turn increase product costs, which must be passed along to the customer. Lack of security is anticompetitive in that it may provide a short-term benefit from lower overhead while at the same time exposing the company to higher long-term costs and exposures.

The only remaining reasonable option for a business is to include security as a component in the management mix in the same way that other expense-related functions are included. Neither can the accounting operations of a business, for example, be ignored. The accounting area can be automated, managed, and even outsourced, but the cost of accounting is a cost of doing business. Most firms have long recognized the cost of accounting and have even elevated the importance of this function to the highest levels of the company with the creation of the CFO role. In some ways, this may be the ideal way to understand security for some companies and why the same organizational model is valid and can lead to the creation of a CISO title.

The other significant organizational issue to review is whether to have a centralized or decentralized security management program. This issue has also been debated many times in many places. The choices are really strategic ones that deal with the overall goals and management style of the business.

In a centralized model, all authority and administration stays in a single, monolithic organization. The manager overseeing security has responsibility for both policy and implementation. The benefits of this model are the ability to identify and manage cost, the ease of decision making, and the simple communication lines between the policy makers and the administrators. The negative side is that this puts security apart from the business side of the company and can be a source of conflict as the business goals and security goals do not converge except at the highest levels of the company. For example, the most efficient way to administer security rights may not be the most user-friendly one. The security staff will optimize its efficiency even at the cost of making the user experience less efficient.

The decentralized model places the administration and implementation roles directly in the business unit and segregates the policy role. Policy usually remains centralized and separate and is linked with other corporatewide roles such as Human Resources (HR) and finance. The benefits of this model are the ability to associate implementation and administration with the business goals and objectives. The negatives are that it creates problems with ensuring that security is evenly administered across the organization and that it is generally a higher-cost model due to the need to duplicate administrative roles across business lines.

Sometimes there is a hybrid that also decentralizes some of the policy role into the business unit. In that model, major policies remain centralized (such as requirements for audit trails, identification of security models, etc.) while others are handled locally. This model works well in companies that have a global presence as it allows for flexible policies that can deal with legal issues, which may vary from country to country.

The decision on whichever organizational model is chosen needs to be controlled and made at the executive management level. It should reflect the organizational goals of the company, the management style of the executive team, and the risk management issues reflective of the industry.

Risk Management Issues Affecting Organizational Models

Another emerging trend in business today is the establishment of a Chief Risk Officer (CRO) position. Currently, this is appearing mainly in the financial services industry in the form of a position that manages credit risk, interest rate risk, liquidity issues, regulatory oversight as well as other management issues. The position interacts with other risk management positions such as auditing and information security and privacy. The goal is to centralize the risk management issues to allow one executive to focus his attention on them with a view to reducing the overall risk exposure of the business. This is an emerging role in business, and other industries will be watching the banking industry to see how well the CRO position works in managing risk.

The risks facing businesses vary somewhat from one industry to another. One of the major differentiating factors is the amount of regulatory oversight that an industry faces. Banking and the financial services industries have some of the most robust risk management programs in place and also have the most comprehensive regulatory oversight programs of any industry. Banks face routine audits from the Federal Deposit Insurance Corporation (FDIC), the Office of the Comptroller of the Currency (OCC), the Federal Reserve Board (FRB) as well as state banking commissions. The healthcare industry is also facing greater oversight and has a number of new regulations that affect its risk profile, including the increasing requirements for protecting privacy. Lastly, public corporations have been brought under greater scrutiny with the Sarbanes–Oxley Act, which, among other things, requires management to sign off personally on the accuracy of all public financial information.

In the past, a large portion of the focus of risk management has been on what could be better called risk mitigation. One of the main ways most businesses handle risk mitigation is through the use of financial controls and financial products that will offset business risk. These include Directors and Officers (D & O) liability insurance, business interruption insurance, and other insurance products. One of the newer products available from the major underwriting firms is E-commerce insurance. These policies are designed to provide a firm with funds to offset losses due to major systems outages. With more and more businesses becoming reliant on systems and network availability, the idea of offsetting some of the risk with insurance products is becoming more popular. This insurance is like all other such policies; it does not eliminate the need to manage the risks or use other means to lower the risk profile, but merely provides a source of compensation for losses. In fact, almost all of the underwriters do due diligence on their customers to ensure that proper measures are in place such as firewalls, intrusion detection, and other preventive strategies.

A list of risk management issues includes ones that had formerly been handled as part of the CFO's responsibilities. The growth in these issues and the increasing complexity has led to the splitting up of those responsibilities and the creation of the newer risk management positions in the executive office. The choices can be complicated by the organizational style and structure of the company. The main issue for management is to decide the amount of visibility that security and risk management needs to have in the company and how best to divide those responsibilities to maximize effectiveness and minimize risk.

Chief Information Security Officer (CISO) Role Defined

The role of the Chief Information Security Officer (CISO) is probably the best known of these newer C-level risk management roles. The CISO usually has the responsibility for developing and managing the information security policies for the company. As stated earlier, in a centralized structure the position will also have the day-to-day administrative role for security management.

The generally accepted list of policies that come with this position are those covering access to information, role-based rules for access and administration, as well as policies governing security labels (secret, public, private, etc.). Some of the responsibility for policies managed by a CISO may be shared with other executives. E-mail policies are frequently co-authored by HR as they deal with issues regarding employee productivity and privacy. There are other areas where HR policies govern behavior, and the policies for content filtering and Web site limitations have similar counterparts in the HR policies governing electronic media. Also, the CISO is usually limited to policies that govern information technology rather than more generalized employee and customer actions.

Typical responsibilities for a CISO include:

- Information security policy
- Privacy
- Network security
- Information technology infrastructure security (mainframes, servers, etc.)
- Computer Security Incident Response Team (CSIRT)

Areas of responsibility that may or may not report to the CISO include:

- Security administration
- Contingency or business continuity planning
- Voice system security
- Fraud prevention and detection

Limiting the CISO to technology-only policies can be the source of some of the management issues confronting the executive team looking at the organizational issues. For example, a CISO is traditionally responsible for selecting the systems that protect access to financial applications. The CISO also sets up the rules for accessing those applications and looks at the systems controls for the hardware on which the application runs. But, when it comes to fraud detection and prevention the responsibility usually shifts to other areas in the organization. Fraud and loss prevention, particularly in the retail industry, are often the responsibility of physical security, even if the means to prevent and detect losses involves technology.

Banks, in particular, divide up these roles even further. Check fraud is still a multi-million dollar industry. Fraud prevention involves a number of exotic technologies, including ones that examine the paper a check is written on, artificial intelligence systems that look at check-writing patterns, and biometric-based fraud prevention systems that use fingerprints or pattern matching for signature verification. All of these systems, though, are usually outside the management scope of the CISO and typically are considered operational issues reporting to the head of bank operations. The actual fraud prosecution may go from that person to the head of physical security; that person generally reports up through the operations side of the bank and not the technical side.

Another area that is often included in the responsibilities of the CISO is voice system security. This is an area that often gets overlooked in small to mid-size organizations until a loss occurs. Voice systems are prone to hacking and theft of services. The service providers are not responsible for the security of on-premise equipment; it is up to the owner to make sure that the appropriate preventive measures have been taken. The reason this falls through the organizational cracks is that telephone equipment may be under the supervision of the network staff or sometimes it is under the management of the facilities staff. The information security area often does not have authority to write policies for voice systems and may not think that this is one of its issues. The hackers, on the other hand, tend to think of voice systems as just another computing device, and are not worried about the internal management issues of their victims. Securing voice systems and other non-IT technology is a good point to begin the discussion over the role of a Chief Security Officer.

The Chief Security Officer (CSO) Role Defined

Looking at the full array of loss scenarios, including physical access, fraud, investigations, and employee screening, is where the role of a Chief Security Officer (CSO) enters the picture. The CSO is an even more recent addition to the C-level model than the CISO. In the past, the duties assigned to a CSO have often been split into several functional areas. Responsibility for physical security, one of the basic CSO functions, has often been assigned to the Buildings and Facilities group, which can be a sub-function itself, usually of the finance area. Other responsibilities such as employee screening and criminal investigations are sometimes outsourced. These diverse roles are all areas to be potentially consolidated under the title of CSO if a company sees the need to centralize control and risk functions.

CSO roles have grown in visibility, particularly since the events of September 11, 2001, and the creation of the Department of Homeland Security. It is noteworthy, however, that most CSO positions are also defined in terms that are more typical of the CISO role, including areas like privacy protection and intellectual property rights.

A way to understand this overlap between the roles is to look at the list of categories defining security management under ISO 17799, a guideline put forth by the International Organization for Standardization. This standard grew from the British Standards Institute standard, BS 7799, which had the following ten key controls for an effective program:

1. A documented information security policy
2. Allocation of information security responsibilities within the organization
3. Information security education and training
4. Security incident reporting and response
5. Virus detection and prevention controls
6. Business continuity planning
7. Control of proprietary software copying
8. Critical record management processes
9. Protection of personal data (privacy)
10. Periodic compliance reviews*

This list is very similar to the list of typical responsibilities for a CISO. ISO 17799 forms the basic standard for measuring a security program. The standard covers the following areas:

- Business continuity planning
- Systems access control
- Systems development and maintenance

*BS 7799, Part 1, Code of Practice. BS 7799, Part 2, Specification for Information Security Management Systems was published in February 1998.

- Physical and environmental security
- Compliance
- Personnel security
- Security organization
- Computer and operations management
- Asset classification and control
- Security policy

A survey published in the magazine *CSO* in April 2003 showed a grade by category for controls from the ISO 17799. The grades in the survey showed that compliance with security was still below 50 percent in most categories at the responding organizations. The highest grades were for physical and environmental security (63 percent average) and the lowest were for systems development and maintenance (43 percent) and business continuity management (41 percent).* The results of the survey are interesting and point out that all the disciplines of an effective security program are not implemented with the same rigor across a given organization. While the standards make a good starting point for the development of a program, what is more important is execution. One of the real keys to execution is accountability, and that comes from the top of the organization.

The ISO 17799 standard makes a good framework for the list of responsibilities for a CSO. Using that list, it appears that a good argument can be made for the CSO role being a superset of roles that includes the CISO. For example, the systems access control function is clearly one that falls in the CISO responsibilities, as do the systems development and maintenance and computer operations and management roles. There are other organization choices, though, and they need to be included as part of this discussion.

Organizational Models and Issues

There are four major areas in the list of security functions that are beyond the scope of a CISO but make the broader role of CSO. These are business continuity planning, physical and environmental security, personnel security, and compliance. The question to be asked of executive management is, therefore, do these functions warrant a C-level role or are there other choices?

At the highest level of this decision-making process is the need to break the policy function out of the management function. In some organizations the CISO role is policy making and oversight. All the administrative and operating functions have been removed and placed in other areas. For example, the administrative role in security management can be seen as an

---

*Human Firewall Council (www.humanfirewall.org) online survey of 1057 organizations done from September to November 2002.

operations-oriented function best done and managed closely with the day-to-day line of business functions. This is a decentralized model and is considered a way to keep accountability closer to the business unit.

A subset of the decentralized model is outsourcing security functions. This is common in the physical security area as many companies use a guard service to manage their physical site access control function. Other security roles that can be outsourced include issuing of security credentials, employee screening, security testing, auditing, remote access systems, firewall management and intrusion-detection system monitoring, and management. The decision to outsource is a complex one and is more fully discussed in Chapter 15. The important issue for this discussion is that there are always residual activities associated with outsourcing such as incident response and vendor management that need to be dealt with by the management team. The decision on where to place those residual activities in the organization is largely the same as the decision would be if they had not been outsourced.

The issue of privacy and protecting information is one that has received much more visibility lately. In some organization this has advanced to the point of creating a position of Chief Privacy Officer (CPO). The duties of a CPO mirror those of a CISO in many ways. The CPO position has a strong policy underpinning and there is a large effort in organizations with major privacy issues to train and educate staff on the policy and how to ensure compliance. This is very similar to the policy functions of a CISO and their efforts to promote security awareness. There is also some overlap in the need to work with marketing and with public relations staff to ensure that the word gets out to stakeholders and even shareholders that the organization is taking the privacy issues seriously. The difference between the two areas begins with administration. Privacy rules typically are a subset of other authorization rules in an IT system. The CISO is usually the role in the organization charged with managing the authentication authorization systems. It is usually not possible to split out administrative functions for privacy from those aimed mainly at protection strategies; as a result, CPO positions are usually more policy oriented by default.

There are many other issues to consider in choosing the right organization model. These include some pressing issues regarding reporting of information to the Board of Directors and public agencies.

Organization Structure and Reporting Models

It may be helpful to look at some sample organizational structures for the CISO and CSO positions. In looking at those models some real comparisons can be made between them, and those comparisons can then form the basis for making a decision about which model to choose.

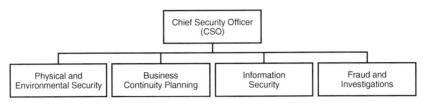

Exhibit 1. CSO Organization Chart

Exhibit 1 depicts the typical CSO organization with a placeholder for information security. In many organizations a C-level person cannot report to another, so this position is shown with that in mind. In this organization, information security is a peer to other security and security-like functions such as Fraud and Investigations and Business Continuity Planning. Organizations such as this typically group all like functions together. By making all the security functions peers under one manager there are some economies of scale in the decision making and in problem escalation. For example, in an information security breach the same people are notified as in a physical security incident. Likewise, fraud investigations often involve teams from the physical and information security areas working together. Thus, this model is operationally efficient. The weakness in this model is that it separates information security from other information technology functions, which can create more of an adversarial view of the problem. This model also does nothing directly to link business strategy to security. Finally, it also puts together groups that may have disproportionate budgets. Information security staff tends to have much higher salaries than physical security personnel, another potential conflict.

Exhibit 2 shows the typical CISO organization. The first thing to notice is that Business Continuity Planning also appears on this chart. This is a throwback to the idea that Business Continuity and Disaster Recovery Planning (DRP) are synonymous. In the early days of information technology, DRP started as the way computers were backed up and protected in the event of an outage. It became customary in most organizations with large data centers to put DRP under the information security department as it was seen as the IT controls function. This view has changed some recently with the move to take a more holistic approach and look at Business Resumption Planning and make Disaster Recovery a subset of that function.

Another consideration has to do with management oversight and reporting. Recent events, in particular the Sarbanes–Oxley Act, have stepped up the role of the Board of Directors and the Audit Committee of the Board. In the expanded role, the Board is being asked to sign off on risk management issues at a greater level of detail than before. This in turn puts pressure on management to increase the amount of information going before the Board

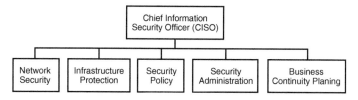

Exhibit 2. CISO Organization Chart

for their review. One way to balance the information to the Board is to consolidate the reporting lines of management. That becomes one of the driving factors in creating a CSO position above the CISO. Consolidating many of the risk management functions into one operating area allows management to consolidate reports and reporting to the Board.

One of the growth industries in information security today is in the area of consolidated reporting, often called security monitoring. Many software companies are producing security management software systems that pull together data coming out of a variety of monitoring and auditing sources. Today, there are many reporting systems supplying a wide variety of information to the information security manager such as audit logs, firewall reports, and intrusion-detection system alarms just to name a few. These reports are generally in a proprietary format and have different goals and uses, making consolidated management reporting difficult. In Chapter 13, the concept of security monitoring is explored in greater depth, touching on the drivers that make up this new product space.

Choosing the Right Organization Model

The previous discussions center on what appear to be a superset and a subset of responsibilities, with the CSO being the superset. There is little literature or even discussion on the reverse topic, that of making the CISO the super manager. That is because, almost by definition, the CISO is just one of the organization's security roles and is by no means the most comprehensive one. The real question remains, however: should there be one position or two? Should the CISO and CSO be peers or should there be a subordinate–superior relationship?

These questions are not ones that lend themselves to a simple answer. This may be a case where the best answer is "it depends." In a large organization with diverse reporting elements, the CSO model will likely be chosen. That model simplifies reporting lines, and the problems of policy creation, management, and enforcement are very similar when looking at physical and information security programs in larger organizations.

In mid-market companies the answer will likely depend on the type of industry in which the business is operating. In a physical asset-centric business such as retailing, the risk management challenges are likely to be more from the physical side of security than from the IT side. Loss prevention in retailing is a multi-million dollar business that requires a lot of specialized knowledge and an investment in equally specialized systems and equipment. In the financial services industry the opposite may be true. For example, protecting information assets and access to financial transaction systems may take up a larger part of the budget and effort in banking and finance. In that industry group there are even further specializations in security strategy for areas such as wire transfer and online banking. The healthcare industry is another one that has its own special needs that bridge the physical and information technology worlds. The current efforts at protecting privacy often involve a mix of physical protections (access control systems) and logical ones (role-based access to patient records).

In the smallest businesses the two roles may naturally join together, again depending on industry. It is more likely, however, that the two roles are really time-sliced roles that managers take on between other duties. The networking manager in a small company often doubles as the CISO, and the owner/operator often doubles up in the role of manager of physical security.

Key questions for executive management in choosing between a CSO and CISO position:

1. How strong are our IT organization's current controls?
2. What is our non-IT financial loss experience?
3. How dependent is our company on IT and the IT infrastructure?
4. Do we have a decentralized or centralized command-and-control system?
5. How closely to our business lines are other operational functions aligned?

The discussion over the CSO role has become a hot issue in the trade journals. In the February 2003 issue of *CSO* magazine, there is an entire article dedicated to a debate between a CSO and a CISO.* The debate in the article centers on the ability of a CSO to expand his vision to include the highly technical world of a CISO. This is largely an academic discussion, but it makes a good way to show how the two roles overlap and how they differ. The center point of the argument is that a CSO has too many other things to worry about to be familiar with the details confronting a CISO. That is the central point of keeping the two roles separate. Without the separation, the fear is that the role of one or the other may be diminished.

That is, however, the duty of the executive management team and one of the areas over which it has complete control. The executive

---

*"Head to Head," *CSO*, February 2003, pp. 29–33.

management team makes similar organizational decisions all the time. Should manufacturing and sales be linked directly or indirectly? Where do you place marketing and public relations on the organization chart? How much authority is placed at the decentralized level and how much is reserved for the home office? Countless articles and books have been written on these subjects, so it is no wonder that the security areas have joined the debate. The questions listed here are a good place to start this discussion, but each business will have its own questions that will need to be answered as part of this process.

In the end, the decision should be kept flexible and be reexamined periodically, as should any other executive decision. The role of CISO as a separate function may make sense today, and rolling it into a larger function of a CSO may make more sense later. The most critical thing for executive management is to examine the roles and duties that make up a CSO or CISO function and make sure that there is someone in the organization tasked with each of those roles; then measuring the performance of that person or persons will fall out of that, and the company will have some level of assurance that it is well protected against the risks and threats that are relevant to its business model.

Section II
Risk Management Topics

Risk management has become one of the most visible roles for executive management in recent years. In the past, this was a topic that rarely appeared on the front page of a business magazine, let alone as the lead story of the nightly news.

Risk management can mean many things in the context of modern business. It can include financial risks, business risks, and technical risks. In today's global economy there are political and legal risks that also have entered the picture. This section focuses on technology and the risks associated with the use of different technologies as they affect a business. There are many ways to mitigate these risks, and each of the chapters proposes ways that management can deal with risk. There is no practical way to reduce risk to zero and still conduct business, but there are ways to mitigate risk and continue to operate profitably in today's global economy.

Chapter 4
Information Security and Risk Management

Introduction

Risk management is one of the basic functions of business. Most information security professionals feel very comfortable when discussing threats, vulnerabilities, and risks from a technical perspective but feel less comfortable when moving to a more conventional business framework. This chapter discusses an approach for the information security professional to use to link the technical view of risk to one that business people are more comfortable with and allow them to better understand each other's needs and issues.

The Information Technology View of Threats, Vulnerabilities, and Risks

There is a common way that information technology people have come to view risks. This forms the background of their approach to risk reduction and minimization. This approach starts with a definition of terms that is based in the Common Body of Knowledge (CBK) that forms the framework of the information security practitioner's world. The accepted definitions of these terms in the IT world are as follows:

- *Threats:* Threats are the sum of all possible things that can go wrong and cause harm to assets. Included in this is the list of natural threats such as fire, flood, and earthquakes as well as man-made threats such as hackers and inadvertent human errors.
- *Vulnerabilities:* The definition of vulnerability is the exposure that the asset under study has to a particular threat. For example, a stand-alone PC is not vulnerable to an Internet worm.
- *Risk:* The intersection of a threat and vulnerability. Attempting to quantify risk is a challenging but important task.

Information security professionals attempt to take this one step further by trying to find a way to quantify the risks so that they can be matched to cost-effective protection mechanisms. The most common approach is to use the following terms and formula:

- *Annual rate of occurrence (ARO):* This is the number of times in a given year that a threat is likely to occur. Each year, for example, the National Weather Service estimates the number of hurricanes that it expects and how many will make landfall.
- *Single loss expectancy (SLE):* This is the dollar amount of losses that a firm can expect from a single disaster.
- *Annual loss expectancy (ALE):* This is the product of multiplying the ARO times the SLE, and is intended to be an approximation of the exposure a firm has from identified and quantified threats and vulnerabilities.

This is not an exact science. There are numerous assumptions that have to be made in this calculation, and as a result this is often seen as subjective and open to disagreement. It is difficult to put a monetary value on information assets such as customer files. A list of zip codes is public information and has zero value, a list of potential customers within a zip code has some value, and a list of actual customers by zip code has the greatest value.

It is also difficult to identify the ARO for many types of threats, as there is not a large body of data available on incidents such as information theft and destruction. Natural disasters, on the other hand, are well documented and there is a wealth of information on the number and type of disasters that have occurred by location and industry type.

The goal of this exercise remains a valid one. Any protection mechanism has a hard dollar cost that is easily identified. The cost of having off-site storage and a disaster recovery center is easy to quantify. The actual risk to any single firm of having a disaster depends on the assumptions made in these exercises. The cost to that firm from a potential disaster is also dependent on the assumptions used and can be open to question.

Business View of Threats, Vulnerabilities, and Risks

The business side of a firm usually has a very good understanding of risk and risk management. Most business people live with the day-to-day balancing of their understanding of risks that they face, and they have developed their own approach to this discussion.

The best example of this comes from the banking industry. Bankers have many means at their disposal to identify and manage the risks that they face. Their whole approach to making money is to balance their return on investment (ROI) against the underlying risks of the assets that make up those investments. They can choose between making loans and investing their funds in less-risky assets such as government-backed bonds. If they decide in favor of making loans, they have a wide array of risk mitigation strategies, including:

- *Collateral:* The assigning of an asset to the loan with the ability to convert the underlying asset to cash to use to pay off the loan.
- *Participation:* The loan can be split among several lending institutions to reduce the risk any one lender would face in the event of the borrower defaulting on the loan.
- *Pricing:* The loan can be priced in such a way that a higher-risk borrower pays a premium for access to funds. This is the idea behind a "prime" lending rate.
- *Reserves:* A general requirement of all banks in the United States is that they establish a reserve for bad loans. That reserve is generally about one and a half percent of the total loans outstanding. The reserve provides a cushion to protect the depositors and investors in the bank in case of bad loans.

All businesses have some similar mechanism for dealing with the risks they face. These mechanisms have the same goal of matching the actual risk against the cost of the protection mechanism that is aimed at reducing the overall exposure from some threat and vulnerability. The standard approach is through insurance, which is a way of assigning that risk to a third party.

The Economists' Approach to Understanding Risk

Economists often use algebra to document their discussions of both macroeconomic (the world) and microeconomic (the firm) issues. When first viewed, this algebraic approach seems to be theoretical rather than practical. It does form a clear basis, however, for this discussion, and it allows both technical and nontechnical people to have a place to start their discussions and then come to an agreement.

This same approach can be used to look at risk in business. The benefit of this approach is that it allows the information security professional to move away from the normal technical discussion of threats and vulnerabilities and view the business as a whole. Information security risks are only a part of the risk any firm faces. Depending on the industry and the product the firm produces, there may be other risk areas that are much greater than those posing threats to the information technology assets.

Total Risk

The starting point of this discussion is to identify all the risks a firm faces; this will be called total risk. This is the Board of Directors' view of the company and it encompasses all aspects of the business. The formula for total risk is:

$$\text{Total risk} = \Sigma(E + T + C + P)$$

where:

    E represents the risks from the general economy
    T represents technology risk
    C represents risks from competition
    P represents risk surrounding the product itself

This can lead to a clearer understanding of the risk picture of one firm or industry vs. another. Looking at the farming industry, the technology risk may be very low, but there may be a high risk from the economy, as farms are usually reliant on borrowed funds. The total risk they face is a balanced one when the economy is stable. The auto industry also faces a high risk from the economy but faces risks from technology and competition as well. Innovation from competitors can create a higher total risk in that industry as has been seen with new products such as sport utility vehicles and minivans. Those new entrants upset traditional manufacturers' plans and added new dimensions to their total risk value.

Each of these general risks can be broken down further into their components. Product risk has a number of components such as materials risk, operational or manufacturing risk, etc. It is important to capture the sum of those risks in order to get the understanding and buy-in of senior management and the business executives of the firm. Once that is done and there is agreement of the overall risk structure, the discussion can move on to the area that the information security professional is most concerned with, technology risk and all its components.

Technology Risk

This chapter concentrates on one risk area: the technology risk. It can be broken down this way:

$$\text{Technology risk} = \Sigma(\text{IS} + \text{I} + \text{T})$$

where:

    IS represents infrastructure risks
    I is the risk to the information being processed
    T represents the risks to the noninfrastructure technology

The risks to the infrastructure of any single firm will vary based on the mix of internal processing and the use of outsourcing vendors. The risks for the noninfrastructure technology, T, are a list of items such as hardware vendors, software vendors, and developers. The degree of risk has changed over the last few years with the growing reliance on the Internet for routine business functions.

Those risks are easier to measure and discuss than the risks to the information itself. A business person expects the IT area to make good choices about hardware vendors and to buy or build the appropriate cost-effective applications to support the business goals and objectives. Identifying a value for those assets is a less complex task. Typically, that can be done through adding together the hardware costs, any purchased software, and the cost of modifying or developing customized software. Those costs tend to be fixed costs and are easy to use in the risk assessment equation.

Working with information assets requires a different approach. Breaking out information risk is important, as that allows this analysis to move beyond the hardware- and software-based view of the world and move into a realm in which business people are more comfortable. Information is a much more complex topic, and the identification of threats and vulnerabilities to the information needs to be looked at as a business problem, not an IT problem. This requires the information security professional to look at his role in the business itself and to work with the revenue side of the company, not just the operational side.

Information Risk

A key role of the business side of the company is to help compute the value of the underlying information. That valuation process can be part of an information classification process or it can be part of the work done in the development of a disaster recovery plan. Either way, it is a role where the business manager rather than the IT manager takes the lead.

This step begins with the identification of the owners of the information. Information ownership is a topic that goes beyond the scope of this chapter, and is explored in depth in Chapter 5. The quick-start approach is to say that the owners of the information are those people in the business who derive revenue from the use of the information. This approach eliminates most operational people from this discussion. Operational control of information assets tends to be custodial in nature. Those assets are needed for tasks in the creation of products but are not viewed as a separate asset. By linking the information ownership role to revenue, you move beyond the idea of information as a means of production and begin to view it as a separate product category. This is important when trying to identify the threats to the underlying information and the vulnerabilities to those threats.

The valuation of information is just one part of this process. The next step is to understand the risks to the information so that appropriate protection mechanisms can be identified and implemented. Going back to the idea of threats and vulnerabilities, threats to information include inadvertent or unauthorized disclosure and misuse. There have been a number of news articles recently that have disclosed cases where thousands of credit card numbers have been stolen from companies. That is an example of unauthorized disclosure of information. The misuse of that information comes when someone uses it for fraudulent purposes. Other threats to information include unauthorized modification, where someone actually changes the information that is stored.

Information has some characteristics that are worth describing. These are useful in understanding the threats and vulnerabilities that make up the risks. Some of those characteristics include:

- *Portability:* Information in most formats is easy to move around.
- *Usability:* The value of information depends on its usability to another person.
- *Shelf life:* Information assets tend to decline in value over time.

Looking at a particular piece of information in view of these characteristics will help the analyst assist in developing a value for the information. It also helps with the understanding of the vulnerability of a particular piece of information. For example, a printed list is not very portable and is accessible only to someone in the same physical location. The same information located on a computer that is linked to the Internet is much more accessible and portable, and therefore more vulnerable to certain threats.

One way to define the threat to information deals with how information is accessed. Information that is on a physical media and stored in a locked vault faces the same threats as information that is stored on a computer. The vulnerabilities are roughly the same in the sense that someone can unlock a vault or access information electronically. The exposure for physical storage should be lower due to the characteristics of that storage, which limits the potential number of people in the immediate area who could have access.

The real vulnerability in both cases has to do with the knowledge of how the information is stored and accessed. The physical aspect of storage in this analysis is covered partly in the noninfrastructure technology risk, T, and partly in the infrastructure risk, IS. This has to do with the medium itself and the use of either attached storage or networked storage areas. What is important is the nature of the risks and how to protect against them in an online or interconnected world.

Information Risk Formula

The formula proposed for describing the risk to information is:

$$\text{Information risk} = f\,(A + K)dt$$

The risk here is the sum of the access to that information that any individual has (A), plus the knowledge of the technology and infrastructure about where the information is located (K), with respect to time (dt). A person with a little knowledge and a little access over time poses a high threat (a hacker attacking a system from the inside or using a guest ID is an example of this threat). Likewise, a person with a lot of access and a little knowledge also creates a threat over time (an insider who explores the system over time can find weaknesses that he can exploit if his actions remain undetected).

One of the critical variables in this equation is time. Most security managers spend their efforts on dealing with access control systems, separation of duties, and classification of assets. Reacting to alerts and alarms may be split between information security, physical security, and audit teams. Time is assumed by all groups to be something they have no control over, and therefore is rarely discussed as a risk. Exploring how different control mechanisms fit this equation is important for the security professional as it can aid him in moving this effort to a more strategic view of risk. Business managers do not need to understand the details of the inner workings of intrusion-detection systems (IDSs) or firewalls. They do need to understand how these systems address the risks in their business activities.

Protection Mechanisms and Risk Reduction

Concentrating on the threats to information, a list of protection mechanisms can be derived and then matched against the major vulnerabilities of access, knowledge, and time. The information security professional is accustomed to looking at these protection mechanisms from a technology risk-matching perspective, and this approach is a means to move that discussion to a more theoretical level to help make this discussion more in line with the way a business person would understand it.

Taking a theoretical approach to this discussion at first seems an unlikely way to get greater understanding from the business side of a company. Usually, theoretical discussions bog down in nomenclature and cause more confusion instead of less. This particular approach has been proven to work through use of it in repeated consulting engagements. It relies on using ideas that are easily understood by the layperson. Access here is a general concept, and the "how and why" of access controls is left out of the discussion. Likewise, knowledge is used as a substitute for a wide array of issues such as the cracker vs. hacker arguments and the issues surrounding knowledgeable insider vs. a script kiddie (a term for a less knowledgeable hacker).

Moving this explanation to the next level requires defining and listing protection mechanisms. Here is where the linkage begins between the threats and vulnerabilities discussed in the opening part of this chapter and the resulting risk to a firm. A list of protection mechanisms for the purposes of this discussion includes:

- Intrusion-detection systems (IDSs), both host and network based, regardless of their underlying speed and methodologies
- All types of firewalls and firewall architectures

- Access control systems, including two- and three-factor systems
- Remote access systems
- Information classification schemes

Excluded in this discussion are specific examples of some common protection mechanisms, including public key infrastructure (PKI), encryption mechanisms, and digital signatures. All of these are specific technologies that have their place in the array of risk-reduction modalities. This discussion centers on the more general terms of access control mechanisms, and specific technical applications fall under those headings.

Matching Protection Mechanisms to Risks

One of the most common complaints of information security professionals is that they lack the full support of management. Almost every book and article on information security policy starts with gaining buy-in from senior management. Those books state and restate the importance of this support and how critical it is to the ultimate success of the information security program.

The next step in those same publications is to address security awareness. There are numerous ideas on education and training for employees and managers, with the goal of increasing their understanding and support of an information security program. If this is not done, the additional overhead required for successfully implementing such a program, such as setting up user IDs, maintaining separation of duties, and classifying information, is seen as interfering with the primary goal of the business. Most managers today accept the need for some level of information security controls in their job, but they may be reluctant to embrace some of the more advanced tools and techniques that the security professional recommends. For example, e-mail ID and password rules are an accepted part of daily life, but content controls may be seen as invasive or overly restrictive.

The goal of this chapter is to create a way to look at the threats and vulnerabilities that matches the protection mechanisms and do so in a way that a businessperson, not an information security professional, would be comfortable with. The result of this matching process is to allow the businessperson to become more comfortable with these systems and to gain both a greater understanding and appreciation for these choices; that should then result in greater support for the implementation of these mechanisms.

Using this formula is a way to focus the business manager on the goal of the security mechanism and away from the technology itself. Being technology focused can cause the discussion to be centered on narrow technical issues. Recent studies by one auditing firm have shown that although over 90 percent of their customers have a firewall, less than one half of the same customers have an intrusion-detection system. Businesspersons do not need to understand the pros and cons of stateful inspection vs. packet-filtering firewalls to appreciate the benefits of having a firewall. They do not need to understand the design implications on network traffic from these choices, as they should be focused on service level agreements (SLAs) that have already documented their needs. What they do need to know is the benefits to the company from having a properly implemented and managed firewall, and how that will reduce the risks the company faces from using public networks as part of its business operations. Further, they need to understand that a firewall forms only one layer of the defensive strategies that are available to protect the company and its information technology assets.

The Risk Protection Matrix

Using the information risk formula, risks can be mapped to protection alternatives. The information security professional can then demonstrate to the businessperson that no single protection mechanism addresses all the risks to information assets and that the best solution is layers of protection mechanisms.

The matrix in Exhibit 1 shows the matching of specific information security mechanisms to the risks posed by access, knowledge, and time. Each of these mechanisms alone can reduce the risk to the information, but only when used together will there be a significant reduction in total risk. Time is the key variable in this equation and it is the one that can significantly increase the risk of the other variables. Controlling access alone without monitoring those controls will not cause total risk to decrease. A hacker

Exhibit 1. Risks and Controls Chart

Risk Variable	Control Mechanism	Comments
Access	Access control systems Remote access systems Password management Encryption	All of these are standard tools for an information security program. They must be properly implemented and managed to be effective.
Knowledge	Separation of duties Security banners Information classification	No single item can control the knowledge of the user but can limit the use of that knowledge.
Time	Intrusion-detection systems Firewalls Bastion hosts Audit trails and alarms Security monitoring	Alerts and alarms that go unnoticed are an additional risk. Implementation of these controls implies the need to manage the alarms that they generate.

doing a brute-force attack on a password can eventually break it if he remains undetected over a long enough period of time. Likewise, an insider can do significant damage to a company if allowed to exceed his authority and his efforts go undetected over time.

Looking at the control mechanisms in this way can demonstrate the need to have an integrated information security program. Buying a firewall alone will not address the risk from giving someone an inappropriate level of access. In a similar way, implementing an access control system without creating a good plan for separation of duties is not an adequate way to reduce total risk.

This analysis can go into greater detail based on the technical knowledge of those involved in the discussion. Access can be looked at from both a physical and a logical side. Some access control schemes require information classification in order to be most effective; others work well with broad classifications of information into categories such as public and private.

There are also other security mechanisms that are not listed in this analysis. Penetration tests, for example, indirectly address these risks as they can identify weakness in the implementation of other security mechanisms. System and file backups can mitigate these risks but do not directly address them. A good security program, however, would have in it system backups and a plan to periodically test the strength of the security systems.

The purpose of this approach is to improve the businessperson's understanding of the risks and threats to information. This is the beginning of a partnership and not an endpoint. By using this formula, the information security professional should be able to advance the knowledge and understanding of his job with respect to the goals of the business. Once that is done the details of the selection of the appropriate protection mechanism can be left up to the security professional, subject to the usual project approval process.

Going back to the study that showed a high rate of use of firewalls and a low rate of use of intrusion-detection systems, the matrix in Exhibit 1 can be used to show the business manager why a firewall alone is insufficient. In the same way, the matrix can be used to show that there needs to be procedures in place to review the alerts and alarms that these protection systems generate. The element of time cannot be eliminated as a threat, but the risk that it poses can be reduced through reducing the time a hacker has before being detected and removed from the compromised system.

Conclusion

The idea of a conceptual approach to understanding risk is not a new one, and one of the goals of this approach is to create a meeting of the minds between an expert and the target audience. Today, as in the past, one of the common complaints of the information security professional is a lack of support from senior management. Books that describe how to build an effective security program all start with the need to have senior management buy-in and then move quickly into creating a security awareness program. What is glossed over in the process is the degree of difficulty in gaining that support.

Using this abstract approach is one tool in this process. Moving the discussion away from a purely technical one and on to a business level is an essential part of this process. Few CEOs are interested in how technology works at the code level. Almost all of them understand the risks and threats to their business plan. By moving the discussion about information security to that same level of understanding, the information security professional will go a long way to increase the support of executive management.

Chapter 5
Establishing Information Ownership

The process of developing an effective information management program begins with first assessing risks and then designing policies and programs to mitigate those risks. One of the critical efforts in the risk assessment process is the establishing of information ownership. Along with that, another important step is determining the value of the information, often through some additional risk assessment process. Risk assessment is usually accomplished through quantifiable means that have been documented and explained elsewhere in security literature. An example can be found in the Appendix of *Computer Crime Techniques,* by Geoffrey H. Wold and Robert F. Shriver,* in which a simple checklist methodology for risk assessment is given. The task of establishing information ownership is usually left to the information security administrator, who often is a staff-level person who may or may not be in the direct flow of the management structure of the business. This chapter describes this process at a more strategic level. It outlines a way for the Chief Security Officer (CSO) or his staff to identify the owners of information in the organization — the key decision makers who will work with security to set the rules for the protection of the business' information assets.

Establishing Information Ownership

Most security manuals touch only briefly on the issue of information ownership. Information is an asset of the organization and is also a valuable resource. Resource owners have been described as the creators of information who are ultimately responsible for ensuring the security of that information. There is a fundamental contradiction in this type of definition because the manager who is responsible for creating a resource can also be the primary user of the information. This situation creates a problem when it comes to evaluating the resource for security purposes; the

*Bankers Publishing, Rolling Meadows, Illinois, 1989.

user of information usually wants easy access to the information, whereas the creator of the information may wish to limit access on a need-to-know basis through some type of security measure.

Determining who can best decide the information's value to the organization is another problem. The creator of the resource understands the pure cost of gathering and developing the information, but the user may better understand the value of the information to the profitability of the business. When they are the same person, the creator and user may have very little knowledge of the true value of the information. A customer-service representative in a bank may gather name and address information yet may not know how much the account associated with that name and address is worth in fees and deposits. Identifying the true owner of this information as either the manager of the customer-service representative or the manager of the branch that services the account may be deemed essential to an effective security program, but it may be a difficult task.

Centralized Information Security

In a simple organizational structure, identifying information ownership can be a relatively easy job. For example, in a manufacturing organization consisting of a factory, a sales office, and a home office, the owners of information are easily identified. The factory manager controls the information concerning work in process, inventory of raw materials, and perhaps even the finished-goods inventory. Payroll information is controlled at the home office because the factory manager is only a user and supplier of information to the database rather than the owner. Similarly, the sales office controls the sales information as well as the receivables system and the data that feeds that system. The respective managers of those areas are the *de facto* owners of the information.

Local Administrators vs. Information Owners

In a simple organizational environment, local administrators can be assigned as a subset of information owners. Although they do not take on responsibilities associated with information ownership, local administrators aid in the security function through awareness efforts and even password administration but are not decision makers in the data security process. They can help administer established security policy but are not makers of the policy.

Local administrators can be assigned to each location that is a separate function in the organization — for example, the manufacturing plant, sales office, and accounting headquarters. The local administrator is responsible for information access controls at that specific location and in turn works with the preestablished owners of the information to form the backbone of the organization's information security system. The owners of information delegate some of the responsibility for the administration of ownership to the local administrators.

Local administrators offer two advantages. First, the concept of ownership is kept separate from physical location issues. Second, senior-ranking persons in the organization who are identified as the owners of information resources can better focus on making policy-type decisions when they can delegate the tasks associated with implementing that policy.

Transferring Ownership

Owners of data can further delegate responsibilities to a surrogate owner. This person is responsible for the daily management of the data, including signing off access requests and making decisions along the lines of authority that have been established by the true owner. Surrogate owners might be used in large organizations, where the owners of resources have various management responsibilities that force them to delegate some of their ownership duties to others.

It must be emphasized that the surrogate owner's duties are separate from the local administrator's duties. The surrogate owner's responsibilities are really ownership issues dealing with the value of the information and the security measures needed to protect the information. In some smaller organizations, the responsibilities of the information owner, surrogate owner, and local administrator may overlap and become the function of a single individual.

Operations Orientation of Information Ownership

The traditional approach, even in a simple organizational structure, has been to identify the owners of information resources through the business operation model. In the banking environment, for example, the head of bookkeeping operations can be identified as the owner of deposit information. In manufacturing, the manager of the factory or assembly line is often identified as the owner of assembly information. This operation-oriented model can be successful when the information flow is centralized and the users of the information are organizationally connected to the operational area. In a simple organizational structure, the roles of local administrator and information owner might be combined in one person chosen from the operations environment.

Information Ownership in Larger Organizations

In some organizations, however, there is a blurring of responsibilities. For example, several factories make subassemblies that feed a single factory that produces the finished product. In this case, the owner of the work-in-process information must be identified for the local administrator of each factory. To complicate matters further, each factory may make subassemblies for different finished products that are assembled in another location and sold by different sales offices of different divisions of the same company. In such a case, the owner of the finished-goods information must also be identified. For the data security administrator, correctly identifying resource owners is the central issue in attempting to use information ownership as part of the implementation of a satisfactory data security program.

Information as an Asset

The importance of information ownership stems from the fact that all information resources are strategic corporate assets. Information is as important to a business as any other asset, and it demands the same type of security measures that have traditionally been applied to other business assets.

Decentralized vs. Centralized Information Security Controls

Many businesses are decentralizing information processing and the controls on those strategic assets. The increased reliance on personal computers as well as the use of mid-range machines and local area networks has also changed the way security is administered. Centralized information security, which worked satisfactorily in the past, has given way to decentralized approaches. This further complicates the issue of correctly identifying owners of information as opposed to users of information.

In a simple business structure — one line of business and one site — controls are easily designed and implemented. As businesses grow and the corporate information resources remain on a central processor, information security remains a relatively simple task that is centrally administered. The need to identify information owners exists, but the owners and users typically are the same people or, at the very least, reside in the same location.

In a widespread business with decentralized data and data processing, there may still be central databases for bulk data but also subsidiary information resources. In addition, the information on the central databases may no longer have a single point of origin but may come from several departments in the business, making the identification of the information owners more difficult.

Establishing ownership becomes essential as information is accessed by more than one type of user. Customers sometimes want access to their information, and third-party processors (e.g., credit bureaus and consulting businesses) provide information to the central database as well as use information off the database for their own processing. Decisions concerning access become difficult as the complexity of the input and output of information increases. What starts out as a simple process of granting read access becomes an exercise in mapping different needs for access and uses for the same piece of information.

Ownership and Information Flow

The current approach to establishing information ownership has evolved from the simple organizational structure. In most large organizations, the same approach is used with varying degrees of success; however, a better approach to identifying resource owners is to examine information flow. Just as raw materials and equipment are assets that can be traced through a company's financial statements, so can information ownership be traced through the flow of information.

Information ownership can be simplified by first understanding the structure of the business, identifying its control points, and using those controls to identify information owners. The key concept to understand is that the owner of a particular information resource should be the person responsible for the functional area affected by that information. Generally, the owner is the person whose department profits from the use of the information. Therefore, by understanding the flow of information as it goes to the profit-and-loss statement (income statement), information ownership can be pinpointed.

Information Ownership Hierarchy

The downward flow of information in an organization begins with its mission statement. A typical mission statement is to "increase shareholder wealth." That mission is documented in the statement of condition (or balance sheet) and the income statement, which are derived from the general ledger system of the organization. Therefore, the ultimate ownership of information rests with the President or Chief Operating Officer of the business; however, the information can be charted as it moves to the corporate financial statements so that the immediate owners of a particular type of information can be identified.

Functional Owners of Information

In a given functional area, the actual owners of information may permit a responsible individual under them who is closer to the preparation, access, and control of their information assets to assume some ownership responsibilities. These individuals are not truly in control of the information but are able to make decisions about its security. Their power is conditional, as they must show that they have authority to act in the place of the true information owner. In practice, their power may be absolute, because the information owner has the authority to delegate all duties. However, the authority for those actions always remains with the actual owner of information.

For example, the company President could designate the controller as the functional owner of financial information (e.g., balance sheet and income statement information). The controller, who is usually responsible for the accuracy of that information, would now also be the owner of that information. All other information exists as a subsidiary of this information. Subsidiary information would also have information owners, who would be the persons responsible for different functional areas.

Generally, owners of income statement-only information and owners of balance sheet-only information are separate and distinct because of the nature and type of information and the source and use of the information. Although there may be apparent overlap, they are and should remain clearly distinct.

Income Statement Information Owners

In viewing information as it flows to and from the financial statements of the company, there are clear ways to distinguish ownership responsibilities. In a typical income statement, the only information owner is the senior manager of the company's sales divisions. Although these areas have assets and liabilities, they are secondary to the sales function, which generates revenue and offsets expenses. For example, a typical sales office has furniture, fixtures, equipment, and receivables listed on the balance sheet. These items are, however, only by-products, not the actual end products, of the work of that division.

The sales manager is a control point because the manager is responsible for the accuracy of sales-revenue information. This is the one person who can clearly quantify the actual value of that information to the organization (as opposed to just the funds it represents). The sales manager is also able to assess alternate ways the information can be viewed that may affect the calculation of the value of the information. For example, forecasts of sales by product may show a steep decline at some point in the future. That may represent a fall in value for a product line or it may indicate an end of a product line and a consequential shift to a new product. That information would be of great value to a competitor.

Information Value

A list of customer names and addresses has more value to an organization than a numerical list of invoices from those customers, even though the latter actually represents the dollar value of business that is conducted. The customer list therefore requires a higher degree of information security. Thus, another key to information ownership is the ability to set the value of the information for the business. This is important because when the information value is established, the cost-effectiveness of the controls can then be evaluated as part of implementing the data security program.

Statement of Condition Information Owners

There may also be owners of what can be called statement of condition (or balance sheet) information. On the asset side are such items as finished goods or raw materials. Asset information is controlled by the head of the production or operations division. If the management of this information resource is handled independently of the direct production of the related income or expense, a separate owner of the information must be identified. That person is the manager of the functional area responsible for the management of that resource, whether it is an asset or a liability.

Duties and Responsibilities of Information Owners

The duties of an information owner revolve around the valuing of the information, determining appropriate controls, and delegating specific tasks and duties as determined by the size and complexity of the business. In a small business, a single individual may handle all these duties. In a larger, decentralized business, these duties may be shared with local administrators and functional information owners.

It is, of course, highly desirable for information owners, who are responsible for maintaining security through appropriate controls, and the data security administrator to work together. The information security administrator might, for example, allow access in a case in which a more prudent level of security, as determined by the owner, would be appropriate. Information security administrators, however, are the persons best able to make decisions about information ownership and how to protect resources. Their efforts cover contingency planning as well. The joint involvement of security administrators and owners is best for identifying critical information and the best means for securing it.

Exhibit 1 is a tracking form that can be used by the information security administrator to document information ownership data. The form lists the name of the owner, area of responsibility, and the type of information for which the individual has ownership responsibilities. The form also has a place to designate custodial responsibilities. A typical information owner may not want to deal with the details of access control and administration of authorization schemes. He may wish to delegate those responsibilities to another area; for example, an operational area that performs the actual data entry and updating of the information systems that contain the owner's information records. This owner–custodian relationship is typically found in large organizations, and the custodian is sometimes thought to be the information owner. Identifying the true owner of information assets will make these relationships clearer and easier to understand. It is

Exhibit 1. Information Ownership Interview Form

Information Ownership Tracking Form

Prepared by: Date:

Information owner name:
Area of responsibility:

Type of information:
Internal (includes product information, pricing data, budget forecasts, etc.):

External (includes customer information, market data, competitive information):

Custodial information:
Custodial relationships:

Custodians' names, contact information:

Applications containing owner's information (list all):

Duration of custodial decision authority (start date, end date):

important to also understand that some owners will want to delegate their responsibilities, and this form can be useful in documenting the details of those relationships.

It may be useful to gather this information first by talking to the owners individually and then later bringing several owners together so they can discuss areas where their ownership duties may conflict or overlap. The advent of Customer Relationship Management (CRM) systems makes this process easier. Using the information in the CRM, the information security administrator can map in a business the different people who use critical information. The CRM may also be a place where ownership responsibilities could be documented once they have been gathered.

Conclusion

A program to identify information owners should be relatively easy if information is analyzed according to its effect on either the company's statement of condition or its income statement. The source of the

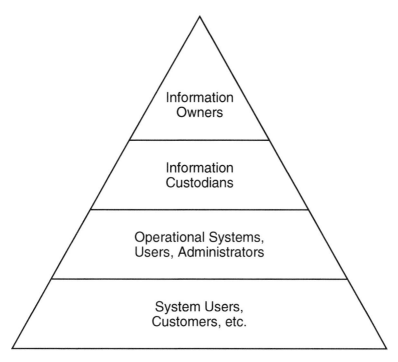

Exhibit 2. Information Ownership Hierarchy Chart

information can therefore be identified; the appropriate manager controlling the information source is then identified as the information owner.

The number of information owners should be limited, although the primary concern is effectiveness. It would be preferable to have multiple owners of sales information as broken down by functional area rather than limiting ownership responsibilities to a single person. Sales information by product type is an appropriate split, as each product may have different security requirements. Too many owners, however, can dilute the power of the ownership, which results in decision-making delays if the various owners need to agree on a common strategy.

Owners need not be administratively responsible to the same organizational level, however. Information flow, not administrative responsibility, should be emphasized. In effect, this method for determining ownership is an inverted tree, with the income statement and the statement of condition at the bottom. The branches of the tree represent ownership points. All the information in the organization comes from a control point flowing to the income statement or the statement of condition. The appropriate security controls are decided at those control points by the information owners.

A graphical way to view this is shown in Exhibit 2. This shows the hierarchy of owners and custodians in an easy-to-understand format.

The need to establish owners of information comes directly from the need to establish the control points for decisions related to securing information. Using this information flow concept, the owners of information can be readily identified and the appropriate security measures developed and applied. The failure to establish ownership will make the successful implementation of a comprehensive data security program difficult. Information owners, once identified, are best equipped to set the value of information and help design the level of protection for an organization's information resources.

Chapter 6
The Network as the Enterprise Database

Introduction

The role of the network has evolved over the past few years from enterprise data conduit to enterprise database. Information technology managers are beginning to view the network not just as a resource, but as an information asset.

Recently, there have been many attempts to redefine the role of the network in computing. Some have suggested that the network is simply a utility, providing services on demand. In this view, the main role of the network is to be constantly available to facilitate enterprise activities. Another view is that the network is the computer, which is to say that the network has replaced any one computer as the central focus of computing. Some information technology professionals have proposed that the network is the print server. This opinion purports that the purpose of the network is to distribute data and then print information on demand, rather than print and then distribute information. The latest change is to view the network as a means of storing and archiving files and information. Storage area networks (SANs) have entered the information technology glossary and have changed the way information is stored, retrieved, and backed up for recovery purposes.

In some ways, all of this is similar to the concept of the network as a utility; in both cases the network is an important piece, but not the focus of information processing. There remains yet another view — that the network is the enterprise database.

A Historical View of Data and Data Management

In order to understand this new concept, it is helpful to review the changes in the views about computing itself that led to this idea.

The traditional view of computing comes from its growth as a scientific/military tool to its use in the 1960s as an operational information system. In the latter role, the computer was used to automate various labor-intensive tasks in business. The classic use of computers to automate

Exhibit 1. Traditional Data Processing Chart

ACME Manufacturing Mainframe Computer

Application:	Payroll
File:	Salary
Data:	Name, center code, position, pay code
Application:	Accounts payable
File:	Vendor
Data:	Part, inventory number, cost

payroll, accounting, and even the census were based on this model. This is still the basic model of computing used in so-called legacy systems today. In this model, the role of data processing is to facilitate operational activities such as reducing cost or speeding up production (see Exhibit 1).

Management Information Systems (MIS)

There was a change in this basic model in the late 1960s and early 1970s that led to the development of the management information system (MIS). This was widely viewed as the high point of traditional mainframe computing thus far. Here the emphasis was on taking the tactical data produced by the operational system and transforming it into strategic information to be used by management to bolster the decision-making process. Information was the key, and the data that already existed in the enterprise was to be transformed into a more useful format.

The advent of MIS brought on some of the first conflicts in modern computing, because the design of the operational system did not facilitate the use of information in this way. A lack of consistent data definitions, for example, still exists in many companies today, as an outgrowth of this problem. Management needed information, not just raw data, and the transformation process was, and still is, often slow and painful.

Information management became more complicated when systems were decentralized and distributed throughout the enterprise. The problem of assembling data into coherent information was then complicated by the data being split into smaller components. Reassembling that into a picture of the total enterprise became an issue of data definition, data location, and even systems compatibility (see Exhibit 2).

Executive Information Systems (EIS)

The final step in the evolutionary process of data was the development of the executive information system (EIS). Migration to EIS is still going on

Exhibit 2. Distributed Data Processing Chart

ACME Manufacturing Plant 1

System:	Manufacturing
Applications:	Inventory, accounts payable, payroll
Data:	Parts, headcount, salary, costs, etc.

ACME Manufacturing Headquarters

System:	Research, product design
Applications:	CAD/CAM, payroll
Data:	Parts, cost estimates, salary, etc.

in most businesses today. Here the MIS, comprised of such traditional systems as general ledger and customer information systems, is taken a step further and combined with sales data, prospecting systems, and competitive information, in an attempt to give management a forward look at where the company should be headed.

The EIS of today are generally developed using downloaded portions of both operational information systems and management information systems, often combining them on the desktop of a client/server type of architecture. This still leaves the computing to be done in its place of origin, and demands that information management be more like a series of heterogeneous activities, rather than the single process that the EIS is intended to portray.

All of these activities are reinforced at the micro level by the underlying computing technology that is in place. File organization progressed from flat files, an outgrowth of the punch card systems that operational systems were developed on, to indexed files used by most MIS. Databases, both hierarchical and relational, are the latecomers, but are also the preferred data structure for the EIS for obvious reasons. Only in the past few years has there been widespread use of database management systems as the backbone of the business (see Exhibit 3).

In many cases, these databases are secondary sources of information, rather than primary sources. They are built on movement of large amounts

Exhibit 3. Database View of the Enterprise Chart

Database name:	ACME Manufacturing
Tables:	Employee_File (designer, assembler, manager, etc.)
	Inventory (part name, number, source, cost)
	Products (name, cost, inventory tag)
	Location_Codes (plant 1, headquarters, etc.)
Data views:	Work in process, cost of goods sold, etc.

of data through the network and are used for query and analysis purposes. In many cases, they represent a way to recentralize data that has been carefully decentralized for other reasons. The fact that they are built this way leads to the nagging issues of data currency and integrity.

The Evolving Network

Networks to transport data evolved in parallel to the evolution of data management systems. The earliest networks were very short ranged, and the centralization of data processes was as much a technical issue as a management choice. As networks expanded and the ability to transport information cheaply over a wider area became a reality, the role of the network changed from simply a transport process to a resource, even an asset.

Airlines were some of the first businesses to realize the importance of their networks to their operations, and their battles to preserve and capitalize on the competitive advantages of their networks are well documented.

In other businesses, the network remained an operational facility, instead of a resource or asset. One manager of a firm was once quoted as saying "nothing beats the bandwidth of a UPS truck" when asked about his firm's intentions for using a network to transmit data instead of mailing tapes. UPS, on the other hand, has realized the importance of its information network and heavily advertises the advantages that go with its network's ability to trace and monitor the shipment of packages.

The network today performs many more tasks than just allowing data to flow. Now the network controls both the flow of information and the access to that information. Network managers are responsible for maintaining constant reliability and for preventing unauthorized users from accessing the system.

Battles over network protocols are really battles about access and flow of information. Incompatible protocols are just as crippling to a business as failed network lines. The growth in importance of the various carriers (MCI, Sprint, and AT&T) can be viewed in some ways as similar to the growth of railroads in the 19th century, because they both have had a major impact on the commerce of their eras. It took standard-gauge track to allow interchange of freight on the railroads, and in the same way it takes standard protocols to allow data to move freely on networks. It is a given that networks have grown in importance, but it is the role of the network within a specific enterprise that gives rise to a new concept.

The Network as the Database

Combining all of this history and evolution leads to a new view — that of the network as the database management system. If one looks at

Exhibit 4. Network View of the Enterprise Chart

ACME Manufacturing

Location:	Plant 1
	Connections: High-speed data transfer
	Low-speed voice/data
Processor:	CPU 1: workstations 1, 2, 3, etc.
Applications:	Inventory, accounts payable, etc.
Location:	Headquarters
Connections:	High-speed data transfer
	High-speed electronic data interchange
	Low-speed voice/data
Processors:	LAN 1, CPU 1, PCs, etc.
Applications:	Payroll, general ledger, etc.

information in the enterprise from the top down, as executive information systems propose (see Exhibit 3), then what you see is that each processing system, whether a mainframe or a single PC, is nothing but a database table (see Exhibit 4). Looking at the network this way, you can substitute the term "database view" for "accessing location X, application Y." A single machine may have unique information, just as a single table in a hierarchical database may have unique data. When all of that data is pooled together, it becomes the total database for the enterprise, and the only place that it exists is in the context of the network that links all the data sources together.

In this way, the network becomes the single most important part of the enterprise's information process. The network, through its role of controlling access and the flow of information, becomes the single place everyone must go to get information. Each processor may stand independently and store unique parts of the database, but the network alone is the repository of all the information. The network, in this model, may be an inefficient database processor, as each view has its own rigid data structure, but the network is the database manager, as it alone controls all access requests for data views.

Network management plays a critical role in the success or failure of a business. Availability of the network becomes an important business function, as does the need to protect the network itself as a strategic asset. It is no small wonder that network security and contingency planning have become such important topics. Single sign-on and cryptography are two of the hottest topics today, and both are related to making information on the network readily available, in a secure manner, to the end user. Likewise, alternate pathing is a major topic in contingency planning for networks.

Alternate pathing is a means to preserve the availability of data in the event of a disaster, if the independent processors survive and the backbone network fails.

Dr. Frank Cullen, co-founder of Blackstone and Cullen, an Atlanta-based software company, suggests another important reason to view the network as a critical information resource.* Dr. Cullen is a leader in developing tools that can access disparate information sources across networks. He believes that it is the ability to infer specific information from different views that has changed the way information technology managers should look at their file structures and access rules to information.

For example, using traditional database tools, access to information can be limited by restricting which data elements a user can retrieve. This is a typical means of protecting information in large databases. User A from company XYZ cannot access information that comes from company ABC. User A can infer that information, though, by requesting a report of the same information that provides "total all information" and a second report that provides "total all information except restricted data" (e.g., company ABC). The reports can then be manipulated to calculate the missing information. This ability to infer high-value information creates a major challenge for the information security program. Prior to looking at the network as the information source, information security managers have been confident that their access control systems are sufficient to restrict access to information. The challenge now is to identify all the sources and uses of information and create a way to protect information as it is valued by the users, not just in the way it is accessed.

Conclusion

Information technology is still evolving today, continuing the shift from tactical, operational systems to strategic, management systems and on to executive information processing. Not only have the application systems, hardware, and file structures changed, but so has the view of the way they function. Networks are even being used by software vendors as a means of distribution and usage monitoring. The evolution of the network to the top of the system hierarchy, where the network can be viewed as the database, is part of this continuing evolution. The view of the network as the database does not change the importance of the other parts of the process; it merely identifies the network as perhaps the most critical resource in the process and calls for the management of the network to become the major issue facing the management of information processing.

*Interview with Dr. Frank Cullen, May 5, 2003.

Chapter 7
Risk Reduction Strategies

Introduction

Risk management for many companies has emerged from the back office to become a highly visible part of executive management. In the past, risk management was thought to be part of every manager's responsibilities. There did not seem to be a compelling reason to have a separate reporting line for risk management, let alone a separate position such as the Chief Risk Officer (CRO) position that some companies are now creating. There have been a number of changes in business and business management that have led to a rethinking of the responsibilities of those running a company. Innovative financial products, privacy laws, and new corporate governance regulations have created the need for more scrutiny and oversight of corporate governance.

In a similar way that new positions such as Chief Technology Officer (CTO) and Chief Information Security Officer (CISO) were created at the higher echelon of the corporation for overseeing privacy, technology, and security, companies are looking at the responsibilities of their executive managers. Risk management is one of the more visible areas that did not have its own executive, although that too has begun to change.

As a result of these changes some companies are naming a CRO as part of the executive team. The reporting structure of this new position varies, although in many cases it is a peer to the CFO. The responsibilities of the CRO are also not yet consistently defined across different industries; however, in general they include financial risk, insurance products (Directors and Officers policies as well as property and casualty insurance) along with other areas such as internal controls and auditing. The idea of a CRO fits in with the more established areas of information technology risk reduction management.

In this chapter, different risk reduction strategies are examined and the pros and cons of their usage are discussed. Creating a CRO position is a decision for the executive management team, but as part of that analysis it is important to understand the different risk mitigation strategies that are available today. Management can then use this analysis to see how those strategies fit with their other corporate goals and decide if it is time to bring all risk management under a single reporting structure.

This discussion starts at the top of the organization looking at the business as a whole and what threats there are to the viability of the business model. There is a progression in the terms "threats," "vulnerabilities," and "risks." That progression comes from ideas in the business continuity realm:

- Threats are events or actions that can have a negative effect on a person or an asset. Viruses, computer hackers, and natural disasters are all threats to a business.
- Vulnerability is the way a threat can be exploited to create the actual loss. When the correct mitigation strategies are not implemented, threats translate into actions that will lead to losses. Computer viruses pose a threat to all businesses that make use of computers, particularly if they are networked to the Internet. Failure to implement anti-virus systems and keep them up to date exposes a firm to the threat and creates vulnerability.
- Risks are the sum of threats and vulnerabilities. Some threats do not apply to a given firm or business, and therefore are not a risk. For example, although computer viruses are a threat, some require certain types of operating systems to be a risk. A virus that exploits a vulnerability that exists only in Windows® operating systems is not a risk to a firm that only uses UNIX-based computers.

Threats translate into risk when there is a probability that the threat can translate into an action leading to a loss or interruption in service.

Information Technology Risks

There is a number of risks to consider in information technology:

- Infrastructure risk, which affects networks, servers, and other hardware devices
- Vendor risk, which covers both the financial viability of vendors and the issues regarding the products they sell and support
- Technology risk, which covers the choices of technologies a business will use as well as the impact of those choices on vendors and products
- Information risk, which deals with the issues regarding the threats and risks to information assets of the business (discussed in detail in Chapter 4 and Chapter 5)

Total IT risk for a business is the sum of these individual risks. This can become complex because of the interactions of the different elements that make up each item. It is helpful to examine each of these risks in depth to understand how a business should manage them.

Infrastructure Risk

Infrastructure risk is perhaps the most complex of these variables. There are risks from the type of infrastructure chosen (network topology, for example), capacity planning, and infrastructure protection (environmental protection, physical protection, etc.) that have to do with management choices made by the firm. There are other threats to the infrastructure that are external to the firm (including hackers and terrorists on one extreme and interoperability and international standards on the other). Dealing with threats and risks to the infrastructure can become very complicated. Chapters 11 and 12 of this book deal with some of the infrastructure risk reduction strategies, including business continuity planning (BCP), disaster recovery planning (DRP), security monitoring, and Computer Security Incident Response Teams (CSIRTs). Each of those strategies is important and should be part of any business' risk management plan.

Vendor Risk

Vendor risk management is not without its challenges. Years ago it was said many times that no one was ever fired for choosing IBM as their primary technology supplier. In that case the choice of IBM was a form of risk management and was a part of a larger risk reduction strategy. Choosing one large vendor for all of IT did not mean that there were no risks; it just minimized the potential impact of those risks by reducing the number of sources.

Vendor risk has many dimensions and one of the most obvious vendor risks is support. Each product comes with a contract that indicates how much support the customer can rely on from the vendor and how long that support will last. If the customer is on the then-current release of a software product, he can rely on a contracted amount of vendor support for that release level. The vendor does not say that the product will always be supported or that the product will not be replaced or superseded by a new release; only that the version in the contract will have a level of support. IBM, in the past, was seen as trustworthy in that there was usually a clear product strategy, and if a product was eliminated, there was a migration strategy made available to the customer for the new product. The remaining component of vendor risk left for the customer to manage was a financial one. How willing was the customer to pay for support and how willing was he to keep the release level current with that of the vendor? In some cases customers updated releases each time a new one came out and in other cases customers availed themselves of updates much less frequently. Although those decisions had a degree of risk associated with them, the risk was seen as part of the duties of IT management made in consultation with the end user. The risks were mainly from the upgrades and from the disruption that the change would cause to production operations.

Recently, some vendors have added to the understanding of vendor risk by outsourcing support of older release levels to third-party companies outside the United States. This adds several dimensions to the decision to stay current with the latest vendor release levels. Now it is not just a question of managing change, there is a political risk to consider when future vendor support is coming from a country on the other side of the globe. One of the traditional risk mitigation strategies for vendor risk was software escrow. By having a full copy of the software available, it was felt that even if the vendor went out of business the customer had some recourse through his ability to take that copy and pay someone directly to provide product support. Now with vendor support potentially coming from another country, the customer has to make sure that the software escrow contract applies to software updated in a foreign county.

Technology Risk

Technology risk is hard to quantify and harder to manage. One of the reasons that there are so many companies providing technology, consulting, and information is the difficulty in assessing and managing this risk. For example, developing a long-range technology plan and choosing a vendor is somewhat of a chicken-and-egg issue. If a company chooses a WinTel (Microsoft Windows on Intel chip hardware) technology strategy, certain vendors are automatically eliminated from the picture. Likewise, choosing open-source software such as Linux eliminates another set of vendors and products. If the decision is to select the software product and vendor first, then there are limits on which platforms can be used. This is a complex and multidimensional process.

As a result, IT executives use many different information sources to help them make such choices. They have to look at the demands of the business side of the company, the availability of applications and services as well as the reputation of the vendors and the long-term viability of the technology itself. Technologies have life cycles just as any other products. There is the early introductory phase, where early adopters begin to try out the new technology and see how it works. Then there is the growth phase, where more and more people learn about the technology and begin to implement it in their business. At that point, other vendors begin to move into that marketplace, offering products that either support the technology or make use of it. Finally, in the mature phase of the technology, almost everyone has adopted it and there are new emerging technologies that threaten the dominance of the existing one. Good examples exist such as the changes from proprietary networks to the Internet, the move from proprietary operating platforms in the minicomputer era to the more open platforms in the client/server space today. This is a constant evolutionary process, and knowing where you are on the product life cycle is one of the keys to effective technology risk reduction.

Information Risk

Information risk is a major issue and is covered in more detail elsewhere (see Chapter 4 and Chapter 5). For the purposes of this chapter it is sufficient to know that there are threats and risks to information itself and appropriate choices can be made to reduce those risks. Those choices often are part of other risk reduction strategies.

Firewalls serve as a good example of how risk reduction strategies interact with each other. Infrastructure risk can be mitigated by the use of a firewall, as a firewall can keep hackers from easily accessing a network. A firewall can be seen as an information protection device as it also protects files and file servers from being accessed by hackers. In either case, what is important is that risks should be evaluated and the appropriate risk reduction strategy should be chosen and properly implemented.

Strategic View of Risk Management

The first step in the process is to evaluate the risks to a specific business. This can be done through a process similar to that discussed in Chapter 12 — business impact analysis (BIA). This process consists of looking at all the potential threats to an environment, identifying the potential for loss, and the potential for that threat to actually occur. With that information in hand it is then possible to develop a profile that will identify the potential loss exposure. That is necessary to evaluate the costs of the protection mechanism and to choose one that matches the risk and loss within the tolerances acceptable to management.

The evaluation of risk is a process that involves both business and information technology staff. The information technology staff is well suited to look at its vendors, the infrastructure, and the technology. The IT staff can assemble the costs of the current information technology investment and can provide forecast about changes in the information technology landscape and how it will impact the company. The business staff can help through providing information about industry trends and directions. Each industry and business line will move somewhat independently along the technology curve. It is the business side of a company that can provide information that is critical to evaluating the timing of changes and movement in the business.

Evaluating threats and the probability of their occurrence is a difficult exercise. There is information available from consultants and industry experts that can help in this process. Actuaries have tables based on long-term experience that can provide insight into frequency of event occurrences and industry averages for losses. This information is particularly valuable for assessing risk from disasters. Other sources include industry associations and vendors. Some of the larger information security vendors track virus and hacker attacks and provide information on the frequency of these events as a public service.

The goal of this information-gathering effort is to build a database that contains investments, future plans, threats, and the likelihood of event occurrences. That information is used to build profiles based on technology, line of business, and products within a company. Once it is available it becomes part of the cost–benefit process in evaluating the possible risk mitigation alternatives.

Alternatives for Risk Reduction

A good model for looking at the alternatives for IT risk mitigation comes from looking at fire protection. Fire protection strategies are among the oldest in business risk management and have been thoroughly studied. The choices are as follows:

- *Do nothing.* This may be the high-risk approach, but it is always a possible alternative.
- *Rely on the fire department.* In a sense this is a form of outsourcing, where all relevant services are handled by a third party.
- *Fire prevention.* In this approach the business owner looks for ways to minimize the chance a fire will occur. This approach can be either low or high cost, depending on how it will be accomplished. Simple methods include making sure electrical connections meet building codes and that flammable materials are properly stored. More expensive alternatives include choice of location and building materials.
- *Fire suppression.* There are a number of ways to accomplish this. At the low end are fire extinguishers; they are cheap, easy to operate, and easy to install. The next level up is a sprinkler system, which is more costly to install, especially if you have to retrofit an existing structure. There are also special considerations for electrical and electronic devices that come into this picture.
- *Insurance.* Insurance is a means of moving some of the risk outside of the business to a third party. Buying fire insurance does not eliminate the chance a fire will occur, it only provides a means to recoup investment or recover expenses in the event of a fire. Insurance has its cost in the form of the premium, which can vary depending on whether or not other measures have been taken to reduce the risk of a fire.
- *Internal fire department.* In some cases the risk of a fire may be so high that the only way to reduce the risk is to have a fire department for private use. This can occur when there are specialized materials or when the community fire service is insufficient to deal with the potential hazards. Airports often have their own fire department on site, for example. Some high-risk factories may also have on-premise equipment to deal with their special needs.

When a business looks at the threat of fire to that business it typically tries to reduce that threat through a mixture of these strategies. Most companies do not rely only on a fire extinguisher or only on insurance; they have both. They may also work hard on fire prevention and have people trained in how to respond to a fire. It is up to the management team to evaluate the threat of fire to the business and choose which strategy is cost-effective for the situation.

A similar model holds true for information technology risk. There are multiple independent risk mitigation alternatives and executive management needs to make an informed decision as to which alternative is best suited for the situation.

Looking at infrastructure risk management, there are some good parallels to the prevention, including:

- *Do nothing.* Just as in the case of fire prevention, this is always an alternative.
- *Outsourcing.* Security can be contractually handled by third parties for everything from firewall monitoring through incident response.
- *Security management.* This involves setting up and enforcing security policies covering authentication, authorization, and system controls.
- *Advanced security products.* This approach uses a broader range of options that are involved in most information security programs; for example, the use of secured operating systems and advanced encryption technologies. This would be typical at many government agencies and high-security firms.
- *Security monitoring.* This involves a proactive approach to collecting all the information available from security systems, devices, and audit trails, and brings them together in one place for analysis and response.
- *Insurance.* There are a number of policies available through major insurance carriers that will cover losses from information technology incidents.
- *CSIRT and forensic analysis.* This is the fire department equivalent, where the company has a team trained and ready to respond to security incidents. The team would have all the tools it needs to perform an investigation and to respond quickly in the event of an incident.

Just as in the case of fire prevention, each of these alternatives needs to be evaluated before the correct one could be chosen. Each business must look at its own situation and make an assessment of the amount of risk that is acceptable and which of the risk mitigation alternatives best fit their needs.

Alternative Strategies for Information Technology Risk Reduction

Looking at the alternatives at the highest level, the choices are to reduce exposure through minimizing risky behavior or choosing a mitigation strategy or both. The behavioral approach is one that should be discussed as a strategic issue. For example, a business can choose not to transact business through the Internet and only use proprietary network connections; that decision will greatly reduce its exposure but also limit its business opportunities. Another choice might be to use a third party for clearing all electronic financial transactions, in essence outsourcing risk to another business. Prior to the Internet, banks provided the majority of such services through an umbrella of activities called Corporate Services. These included the use of wire transfer systems, Automated Clearing House (ACH) transactions, and other electronic payment systems. The banks accepted all the risks for the payment processing and the customers were charged fees for the services. The rise of the Internet has created an alternative to those services and fees, particularly for smaller businesses.

Other nontechnical ways to reduce exposure include having better controls in the areas of choosing whom you do business with and doing more research on new employee hiring. There are companies, such as Choicepoint, that have harnessed the power of the Internet to provide automated employment screening, thereby reducing the risk of hiring the wrong person. Once a person is hired, many companies now also have the employee sign compliance statements acknowledging his responsibility for policy compliance.

Reducing exposure alone does not completely address the risks facing a business. It is up to management to do its part in looking at industry best practices and seeing that the company is living up to its fiduciary responsibilities. Management has to look at the mix of business, the way that funds will be handled, and how it all is tracked and reported. As part of that process, management should review technical and administrative controls that will help to reduce risk.

For information technology risk the list of alternatives include access control systems, application controls, network protection (firewalls, intrusion detection), and audit systems. The breadth and depth of the controls will vary based on a number of issues. In general, these controls do not exist in a vacuum and can be thought of as linking together to form a complete protection system. The network protections come first, then the operating systems must be protected, and finally the applications themselves must be protected. In some ways, this begins to look like the seven-layer Open Systems Interconnection (OSI) model:

1. Application
2. Presentation
3. Session
4. Transport
5. Network
6. Data link
7. Physical

The OSI model is used to describe communications protocols and how they interact with each other. It is possible to create an abstract version of this model, which is very useful in looking at risk reduction strategies. There are a "what" (application, presentation, session) and a "how" (physical, data link, network, and transport) in this abstract view. Each information technology management team, working with its partners on the business side of the organization, needs to evaluate the "what" and "how" that business will be conducted and then select the appropriate risk reduction strategies. If the business will be conducting a large volume of financial transaction processing using public networks, then message protection becomes the major goal of risk reduction. That can be done through use of a variety of common information security policies and tools such as authentication systems, authorization schemes, and encryption. If, on the other hand, the system in question is only used for product development using test information, then privacy protection (ensuring that the test information cannot be confused with production) may be more important than the other requirements.

There is a wide variety of information technology risk reduction strategies. As indicated in the previous example, many of these are well known and widely used. Most users are very familiar with authentication systems as they sign onto their computer or network with the familiar user ID and PIN. Other strategies include authorization systems and information classification (public, confidential, secret) systems. There are some risk reduction choices that are less familiar to business executives and even to some information technology professionals.

Trusted operating systems do not get a lot of press. In the United States, these are an outgrowth of research done for the Department of Defense (DoD). In a book that came to be known as the "Orange Book" (because of the color of the cover), the DoD wrote specifications that described the degree of trust that would occur in operating systems. The Orange Book specification described commercial-grade systems as "C" level; for higher security, there were the "B"-level trusted operating systems. The B2 specification described a trusted system with compartments that did not allow user rights and privileges outside of each compartment without expressed permission. In the commercial system, users can have privileges that allow them to read, write, or update in any area of the system. One of the ways a hacker succeeds is by hijacking an authorized process and using the rights of that process to run unauthorized programs. This is sometimes called inheritance and is the way that a hacker exploits programs that can overflow a buffer area in the operating system. That would not occur in a B2 operating system because each process has to be separately authorized and inheritance is not possible. There are available today several commercial versions of trusted B2-type operating systems. These tend to be more difficult to use than their commercial-grade counterparts, but the benefit is they are much more resistant to attacks by hackers. These systems are not well known because they can be difficult and costly to implement. They are mentioned here to further the point that strong security protection comes in many different packages, and that developing a comprehensive risk reduction strategy will involve looking at the entire landscape of both business processes and solutions before choosing the right alternative.

There are other, newer ideas being proposed that will provide additional levels of protection and risk reduction. Microsoft is also working on this problem and has come forward with a new idea called the Next Generation Secure Computing Base (NGSB). This is based on an earlier project called Palladium, which Microsoft and Intel had proposed. This idea is similar to the concept of a trusted operating system and is designed to only permit authorized programs and processes to run. It will block viruses, worms, and Trojan horses from executing as they typically masquerade as authorized processes after gaining access to a system. The NGSB system would query each program or process and execution time, and challenge its authorization. Because the virus or Trojan horse does not appear in the authorized list, it would be rejected by the operating system before it could run and do damage. Microsoft has also said that this will be tied into its efforts at Digital Rights Management (DRM), making this a controversial proposal. This is a new initiative that will take several years to enter the marketplace.

There are also nontechnical approaches to risk reduction, some of which have been in use for a long time but may not have been thought of by most people as risk reduction alternatives. One of the more common ones is what could be called the validation of a business partner. In the traditional business setting, this is standard due diligence. In a contractual arrangement, both parties will investigate each other through the use of credit bureau information or through checking on references. This is done prior to the execution of the contract, even though a well-written contract is itself a form of risk mitigation. In the realm of technology, this validation process may include use of third-party certification that the service provider is performing within industry standards for security and contingency. There is an older form of this type of certification, the SAS70 review. These appraisals are a traditional information technology analysis performed on a vendor by a third party, typically an audit firm. In an SAS70, the third party is certifying that the service provider is performing its duties correctly within the limits stated in the review. Information technology service providers will give a copy of their SAS70 review to customers, and that document serves as another nontechnical form of risk mitigation.

Recently, some firms have begun to take this process a step further, insisting on additional certification of the business partners. Companies such as Choicepoint and Equifax insist that prospective customers provide a certification by a trusted third party that the customer meets a level of care for information security. The requirements are proprietary and the frequency of the review is up to the service provider, making it a more controllable process for them. A client that refuses to provide the proper certification will not be allowed to do business with either Choicepoint or their peers. According to William Esterhuizen, CIO at a peer company, potential customers wanting to access sensitive information online must pass a rigorous examination by third-party experts prior to being given access. The third-party certification process is repeated on a regular basis so that it reflects the current situation with those business partners. Esterhuizens company believes strongly in this form of trust as a means of protecting both its systems and the information that it holds in a custodial relationship for thousands of consumers and businesses.

The problem with this approach is that it can lead to the balkanization of the certification process as each service provider may require a different list of security standards for compliance. If each company defines compliance in a slightly different manner than its peers, it becomes increasingly difficult to say a firm is compliant and therefore trusted. The idea is interesting, however, as it combines information technology controls with contractual ones. It closes the loop on the process, making responsibility for security a shared goal between customer and service provider.

Choosing an appropriate risk reduction strategy is an open-ended discussion. The senior executive in a business should be involved in the final recommendations, and should understand the alternatives and what it means to choose one over the other. It should be up to the management of the technical staff to handle the detailed requirements for interoperability and to choose the appropriate vendor.

Evaluating the Alternatives

The different risk reduction alternatives should be presented to management in similar formats for ease of comparison. This will allow senior management to make the choice based on quantifiable data as opposed to opinions. This usually starts with information such as purchase price, implementation and support costs, vendor name, vendor analysis (vendor financial information, references), and any other hard facts that are part of the decision process. Comparing one alternative to another at this point is based mainly on hard data, and then the analysis shifts to looking at functionality and more subjective measures.

This may not be a simple process and it may take looking at the alternatives from different perspectives. To review the alternatives, each business line will have to answer some questions from the team doing the analysis. A likely list of questions may look like this:

- Will the system have internal users, external users, or both?
- What is the size and frequency of messages processed by the system?
- Will the Internet be used?
- Do the messages need to be protected against interception and modification?
- Is the application a commercial off-the-shelf (COTS) one or has it been developed internally?

There are many other questions that will come up as part of the evaluation process. Each business line will be surveyed and the results will then be collected and consolidated. The answers to these questions will then help in choosing the best protection method.

For example, the list of requirements for one business line may include:

- *Strong privacy protection.* A way to ensure that no one but the sender and receiver could read the message.
- *Message authentication.* A means of proof that the message was as described.
- *Non-repudiation.* Proof that the message came from the person who appears as the message author.
- *Volume.* Low volume but long message length.

A different business line may have these requirements:

- *Proof that the message has not been altered.* Some way to show that the message sent was the same as the one received.
- *Volume.* High volume of messages with short length.
- *Timely delivery and receipt.* Time is of the essence, and delays in message delivery and processing can result in financial or regulatory penalties.
- *Source route information.* Some definitive way to show where the message came from and what other places it may have traveled.

The first business line might be best served by using public key infrastructure (PKI), because that is one of the security methodologies that provides non-repudiation as one of its benefits. The second line of business might be able to use Secure Sockets Layer (SSL) protection, a common format of Internet protection.

Exhibit 1. Risk Assessment Interview Record

Prepared by: Date:

Department name:
Contact name:

Description of business line:

Transaction descriptions:

Size:

Volume (transactions per minute per hour):

Format:

Information formats:

Loss potential:

From:
        Message interception:
        Modification:
        Repudiation:

Other risks posed by business line:

As each business is reviewed there may need to be compromises made in selecting the best alternative. This will require the team to go back to the original source and ask what requirements can be changed or which risks can be offset with other protection mechanisms. Here is where looking at all the alternatives, technical as well as nontechnical, is important. Exhibit 1 is a form that can be used for collecting information of business risk. The loss rating can be either dollar values, if those are known, or something more generic such as high/medium/low. The important point is to gather this information at the front end of the process and collect it from all business units to get a consolidated view of the business.

The other dimension for this decision has to do with the estimation of loss expectation as part of this process. There have been various ideas about how to estimate potential losses and damages, and this will also vary by industry type and company. The estimates will not be precise and are most useful for comparative purposes when looking at protection alternatives and business line comparisons. Here is an example of the loss estimation process:

Problem: What is the business impact of a temporary loss of service for an online store?

Computation:

Average transaction: $25 gross with net income of $2.50

Number of transactions per hour: 100

Net income per hour: $250

Estimated losses for a four-hour service interruption: $1000

Estimated cost to restore service:

Hourly rate of service technician: $50

Number of technicians involved: 2

Cost of repair (two employees @ $50 per hour for four hours): $400

Total estimated cost of incident: $1000 + $400 = $1400

The estimated loss here does not cover other impacts, such as customer confidence or other nonfinancial impacts. The other key variable is to estimate the number of incidents that might occur per year. That information then provides an estimate of annual loss expectancy (ALE), which can be used in evaluating risk reduction alternatives.

There are other potential costs that should be evaluated, including potential legal liability, reputation risk, and regulatory issues, each of which must be reviewed and added into the mix. In some cases, there are penalties from business partners for failing to process transactions within certain time limits. The credit card industry has such penalties in contracts with the various card issuers and processors. In other cases, liability for fraudulent transactions may shift from one company to another in the transaction flow based on the inability to promptly verify the cardholder in a transaction. These costs should be estimated and added to the analysis.

The next step is to look at all of the potential risk reduction alternatives. These include authentication schemes, network security alternatives, and even insurance products. For most businesses, this list will be short and will be similar across the different business units. Network protection alternatives (e.g., firewalls, intrusion-detection systems) will be shared by all lines of business as will more expensive alternatives such as PKI. Business continuity planning alternatives such as hot sites and alternative network routes are also shared expenses. It is important to gather a list of the alternatives and make sure that all threats have been matched to some mitigation strategy. The final part in the management task is choosing between these alternatives and implementing the ones that are appropriate.

It is not the intent of this book to go through all the alternatives in detail. Risk reduction alternatives are continuing to evolve rapidly, and the material presented here could easily become out of date. The important point to make is that these are business decisions that should be made with input from the technical side as well as from the business side of the house. Just because the answers are complicated and the alternatives may be highly technical in nature does not mean that executive management should allow this decision to be made without its input. The success of any of these choices is dependent on the support of management and the commitment of the resources needed to make things work.

The other key issue facing executive management in this discussion is to understand that there are nontechnical risk management alternatives available. It is up to executive management to insist that all alternatives should be put on the table as part of this discussion. Only when all the information is presented can the right decision be made. In some cases that may mean accepting risk with minimal protection, and in other cases it will mean using all technical and nontechnical means available to reduce risk to an absolute minimum.

In some cases, to return to the analogy, it will mean doing nothing, and in other cases it will mean having to own a fire department. The decision is for the business process owner to make once all the risks and risk reduction alternatives are known. You do not need a fire department to protect a low-value commodity-type asset, but you may need one to protect the crown jewels of the organization.

Chapter 8
Improving Security from the Bottom Up: Moving Toward a New Way of Enforcing Security Policy

Encouraging Personal Accountability for Corporate Information Security Policy

The goal of information security professionals through the years has not been to just get policies written but to also get compliance. They have long sought additional support in enforcing the information security policies of their companies. The support they have received has usually come from internal or external audit and has had limited success with influencing the behavior of the individuals who make up the bulk of the user community. Internal and external auditors have their own agendas and do not usually consider themselves as prime candidates for the enforcement role. The security professional has had to look around the organization trying to find the right person to help with the enforcement issue. This problem has become even more complex with the growth of Web-based applications and the resulting large increase in the size of the user community.

Other attempts to achieve policy enforcement have included rounding up the usual suspects of senior management pep talks, executive management memorandums, and security awareness campaigns. In general, none of these programs have been perceived as successful as evidenced by routine tests of information security policy compliance. For example, Pentasafe Security Technologies recently conducted a survey of over 1000 employees in over 350 companies that said that 70 percent of the companies had failed to follow up with employees who had not signed off on the corporate security policy (see www.pentasafe.com for details).

This chapter discusses a new approach to enforcement of policy, one that seeks to move the issue along to become part of the everyday responsibility of both management and employees. The proposal is to encourage the support for these policies by moving that role to the employees of the organization through incorporating compliance activities with the annual personnel performance evaluation.

Background

The successful implementation of an information security program comes through a combination of technical and nontechnical efforts. The process starts with the development of a comprehensive plan that assesses the risks and threats to the individual firm. The next step is the development of a set of policies and strategies to mitigate those risks. These policies are often a mix of physical, technical, and nontechnical items that require routine testing or measurement to ensure that the desired level of compliance is maintained over time. The final steps of this process are monitoring and enforcement of policies and procedures.

Examples of the specific policy approaches to implementing a strategy include:

- *Physical security:* Fire protection, access control systems
- *Technical security:* User IDs and passwords, firewalls and intrusion-detection systems
- *Nontechnical:* Policy manuals and awareness programs

The traditional approach for information security professionals has been to start with the policies that address technical issues, and this is often done in cooperation with the information technology staff. Examples of policies that are mainly technically focused include installation standards (changing default system user IDs), requirements for use of firewalls, turning on of system logs and audit trails, etc.

The next level up in the approach is usually the realm of what is now generally called identity management — the specification of authentication and authorization for the accessing of information and resources. This approach is a broader-based one and it expands to cover a multitude of related policies for things such as password standards, password maintenance, and remote access to networks and systems.

The Problem

In the past, it appeared to most security practitioners that the bulk of their problems were internal rather than external. Whatever their level in the organization and regardless of the degree of support they feel they have or do not have within the organization, it has become clear over time that Pareto's law applies here: 80 percent of the problem is caused by

20 percent of the people. In a recent CIS/FBI survey, the top-three reported sources of financial loss were viruses, laptop theft, and Internet abuse.* Of those three issues, Internet abuse and viruses can be generally mitigated through the development and enforcement of appropriate security policies. For these policies to be effective the staff of the organization must adhere to them. Prohibitions against opening unscanned e-mail attachments and surfing the Internet are both items that have long been part of the basic policy set of the security practitioner, yet they consistently rank 1, 2, and 3 as the major sources of loss for organizations.

In a recent Pentasafe Security survey, it was found that nine out of ten employees were likely to open and execute an e-mail attachment without questioning its source or authenticity. This leads, of course, to virus and worm infections on the corporate e-mail server. Why do people do this, despite the widespread publicity that such infections have received? Is it lack of awareness, as some may say, or is it lack of understanding of the consequences of failing to comply with security policy?

Companies have tried a variety of means to ensure that their employees have received at least minimal training in information security policies. Following is a list of some of those approaches:

- Inclusion of security policies in employee handbooks
- Requirement to take a self-study course prior to initial issuance of user credentials
- Annual testing of security awareness
- PR campaigns using posters, Web, and e-mail reminders

All these are valid approaches and should be considered as a part of the security program for any company. Yet despite these types of programs, security practitioners still find that users fail to perform routine functions such as choosing passwords that are not easily guessed or even shared, for example. Raising the bar on having complex passwords that must be changed frequently often results in passwords that are written on notepads and left beneath the keyboard.

According to press reports from a May 2002 conference sponsored by the National High Performance Computing and Communications Council, several speakers urged stronger user-awareness programs and more involvement of top management. These two concerns are brought up again and again around the industry.

When employees are interviewed about their lack of compliance, they often cite the pressure to be productive and state that they see the incremental security policy as counter to their productivity. When it comes to

*Computer Security/FBI survey of Computer Security Issues and Trends, CIS/FBI 2002, p. 13.

complying with security and trying to be productive, most users err on the side of productivity rather than security. This leads to the question of how one makes employees personally accountable for their role in compliance with information security policy.

Some security professionals say the problem starts at the top with a lack of awareness and support by the executive team. There is some truth to that, as the budget and resource allocation starts at the top; and if there is no money, there is little chance that the security program will succeed.

> *There was a recent survey in 2002 by PricewaterhouseCoopers of 1000 companies in the United Kingdom. The survey found the majority of companies spent on average less than one percent of their total IT budget on information security while an average three to four percent was recommended.*

> *Paradoxically, it said 73 percent of senior managers interviewed believed that IT security was a top priority.*

> *The survey was commissioned by the Department of Trade and Industry.*

Many alternatives exist that can improve security in a firm. Money alone would help, but funding is only a means to an end. To meet the goal of improving security, visibility and enforcement are also major concerns. In its 2001 Industry Survey,* *Information Security Magazine* ranked budget concerns as the number-one obstacle to security, followed by lack of employee awareness and management support. None of these are new findings, yet year after year they remain among the top concerns of security professionals.

In some companies, a new approach emerged in the late 1980s in response to the desire to elevate the issue of information security, i.e., the creation of a "C-level" position for security, Chief Information Security Officer (CISO). The thinking was that by making the position a peer of the other C-level positions it would be easier for that person to gain compliance with policies. Giving the CISO a seat at the table would put the individual in a better position to ensure that security policies had the full support of the management team.

The Role of the Chief Information Security Officer (CISO) in Improving Security

Recently with the increasing awareness of security from incidents such as the Code Red worm and the Melissa virus, there has been resurgence in the movement to create the position of Chief Information Security Officer (CISO). The emphasis on privacy issues brought out from legal and regulatory initiatives such as the Gramm–Leach–Bliley Act (GLBA) and the Health

---

Information Security, October 2001.

Insurance Portability and Accountability Act (HIPAA) have brought about another innovation: the creation of a Chief Privacy Officer (CPO) position either in addition to or instead of a CISO. Although some firms have done this to be leaders in the movement, all too often this has been done due to poor results shown in audits of existing policies and compliance. The higher-level reporting structure is seen as a way to better ensure that information security receives the proper level of management attention.

The financial services industry is usually cited as the leader in information security compliance. Based on published reports such as a July 2002 General Accounting Office (GAO) finding of weaknesses in the security program at the Federal Deposit Insurance Corporation (FDIC), the creation of the new position alone has not been shown to be the way to ensure policy compliance across the enterprise.

Centralized Management vs. Decentralized Management

Many companies today have some form of matrix management in place. In one company the Chief Security Office had responsibility for security policy from both a creation and enforcement standpoint, but he only had a dotted-line responsibility for the tactical side of information security. In that company, the technical policies were done first by and for the IT department and then rolled out into either the employees' manual or the enterprise compliance manual. It is this set of policies that become the more difficult ones to assess and to ensure compliance despite their corporatewide distribution.

This split is not atypical today. Another alternative is to split out security administration from security policy and management. The responsibility for administering passwords and user credentials is often part of the technology area. In other cases, these responsibilities may even go to a network help desk for administration or it may become an automated function on a Voice Response Unit (VRU).

There may be nothing wrong with either approach, but the measurement of compliance with policy is often overlooked in this case. The security administrator's performance may be measured by things like password resets and log-in failures, but who is measuring why those passwords need to be reset and who is responding to any audits of the strength and quality of the passwords? Who is doing the follow-up in the remote business unit to understand why policies fail to achieve their goals?

Security Policy and Enforcement Alternatives

One of the standard descriptions of an information security program is that it is about "people, policies, and procedures." In developing the policies for a company, this is taken down to the next level, and process is then about creating a risk profile and developing the appropriate policies to reduce risk. Once the policies are created the appropriate implementation mechanisms are put in place, after which come the controls that allow the measurement and enforcement of those policies.

Technology-Based Enforcement

For example, the risk profile of a company with product trade secrets will logically be different than the risk profile of a company that is in the services business. The company with the trade secrets has high-risk information that needs to be kept secure, and it may have a detailed information classification policy as part of its Information Security Policy manual. Along with information classification, it may also have role-based access controls that allow it to implement the classification policy. This then may lead it to the implementation of certain technologies that allow automated controls and enforcement of the information classification and access control policy. This can then be described as technology-based enforcement. The access control system once properly implemented allows or prevents access to information and enforces the policy.

There are many good examples of this approach in the marketplace today. This approach sometimes comes under the title "Identity Management." It addresses a broad spectrum of controls, including authentication and authorization systems (see Chapters 9 and 10). Included here are such technologies as biometrics, smart cards, and more traditional access control systems. Enforcement is done through approval or denial of access and reporting of policy violations through error or audit logs.

Executive Enforcement

Frequently cited in articles on the creation of an effective information security program is the need for support by executive management. This sometimes is seen as the route to enforcement of policy. Comments heard from many IS professionals include "I need the president of the company to come out in favor of our policies, then I can get people to comply with them." There is a fallacy here as executive management is too far removed from the day-to-day operations of a company to become enmeshed in the enforcement of any given policy. It is unlikely that the president of a large or even medium-size company can be brought into the discussion of the virtues of maintaining role-based as opposed to broad-based access controls. This type of discussion is usually left to the operational areas to work out.

It is possible to get the support of the executive team to send the message to all employees about their support for information security. That executive support can, in fact, be essential to the IS department as it spreads its message. It is very difficult, on the other hand, to translate that support to direct action on the enforcement of specific policies.

Audit as Enforcement

The auditing department of a company is often believed to be part of the enforcement mechanism and sometimes maybe seen as the primary enforcement tool. Most auditors disagree that they should play an operational role and try to keep their "enforcement" role to a minimum. This is often done by auditing the existence and measuring the effectiveness of the policy, and leaving the role of enforcement to others. For example, the auditors look at whether or not there were policies governing role-based access to classified information. They then may drill down and test the effectiveness of the administration of such policies. The findings would be of facts: "We tested the authorization policies of the XYZ department. We found that ZZ members of the department had complete read, write, and update authority to the system. This appears to be inappropriate based on the job description of those people. We recommend that management review the access list and reduce it to the minimum number of people necessary to perform those critical job functions, and that access be granted based on the job description on file with the HRMS department."

This type of finding is typical of most auditors' role and does not lend itself to assisting with the enforcement of policy. For example, in this case there is no finding that indicates who created the violations nor is there a finding of what actions should be taken to ensure that the guilty party be admonished for creating the violations.

Traditional Managerial Enforcement

The remaining place that most people look for enforcement of policy in an organization is the individuals managing the various corporate departments. Enforcement of information security policies here comes under the broad heading of enforcement of all corporate-level policies. Managers, like their employees, have to juggle the sometimes conflicting need to enforce policies while maintaining productivity. Sometimes employees see the need to have access beyond their normal approved level as a means to improve their job performance. In other cases, there may be conflicting messages sent by management about which goals of the company have priority. In any case, this model is one of distributed enforcement that can lead to uneven application of policy and compliance. No two departments or divisions may see policies in the same light and enforcement; it is then a matter of individual taste. A senior bank examiner once described this approach as a confederacy as opposed to a federalist system.

All of these methods have been tried through the years with varying degrees of success. Few people active today in the information security field have great confidence that their enforcement mechanisms are working to their satisfaction as evidenced by the results of the polls that continue to cite management support and buy-in as one of the top-three obstacles to security.

Policy Compliance and the Human Resources Department

A security manager at a large, multi-national firm was recently asked if it would make any difference if security compliance were to become part of the employees' annual performance assessment process. "It would make all the difference in the world," was the response. The Human Resources manager of the same firm was asked if his department could help enforce information security policies and his response was "no way."

The HR manager explained that, to his department, policies were a zero-sum game; if a new policy were to be added, they would need to consider which policy to drop. They understood that compliance could become one of their responsibilities, and they already had to measure compliance with policies covering attendance, hiring practices, privacy, pay equity, and a host of others. Which policy should they drop to help with the compliance to security policy?

They had a good point when asked what would happen if compliance to security policy was added as a job performance criterion. Suddenly there was a change in attitude and an understanding that perhaps a middle ground could be found where compliance and enforcement could be brought into existing policies and procedures.

The problem then is how to accomplish this and how to maintain the support of the Human Resources professionals. The remainder of this chapter explores this idea and proposes a possible means to accomplish this through the development of an annual, personal information security plan by each employee.

The Personal Security Plan

The HR people in that firm gave a glimmer of hope that security could become part of performance appraisals, and therefore compliance with policies could not only be measured but could be enforced at some level. Most employees understand the old adage that what is measured gets done. If the company provides a way to report on its compliance with any policy and links it to performance measurement and compensation, then it is more likely to comply with that policy.

Personal Accountability

A new phrase has popped up recently in the press with respect to IT practices — accountability. This has come up with some of the recent legal actions where victims of poor IT practices are filing suits against companies that may not have perpetrated certain acts but failed to protect clients. There was a recent action where a denial-of-service (DoS) attack occurred and a lawsuit was filed against an Internet service provider (ISP). The ISP's network was used by the perpetrators to launch a so-called zombie DoS attack; a zombie attack occurs when code is inserted on machines that allow a third party to launch an attack from those machines without the owners' approval. This case is still moving through the court system and the outcome at this point is undetermined, but the net effect is to shift the burden of blame to people who fail to practice safe computing. This philosophy can then be used in another way to help shift the focus of enforcement of policy from local department management or audit of technology to the individual. Making the individual accountable for compliance with corporate policy makes it the concern of everyone and removes the issue from one of selective enforcement.

This idea received a boost recently with the backing of professionals in the U.S. government:

> *Federal agencies must raise staff accountability for breaches and demand security becomes standard in all network and computing products. Otherwise, enterprises will not be able to improve cyber attack response and prevention, according to highlights of a recent conference sponsored by the National High Performance Computing and Communications Council.*
>
> *Rather than emphasizing technology's role in information security, several speakers urged stronger user awareness programs and more involvement of top management.*
>
> *"You can't hold firewalls and intrusion detection systems accountable. You can only hold people accountable," said Daryl White, chief information officer for the U.S. Department of the Interior, in a published report (emphasis added).* *

The Personal Security Plan: Phase One

Using this approach, the proposal being made here is the creation of a personal security plan and the incorporation of that plan into an employee's annual performance appraisal.

Exhibit 1 shows an example of such a plan. This is a simple document that addresses the basic but core issues of security. It is not highly technical nor does it require the company to invest money in any large-scale implementation for technical solutions such as biometrics, public key infrastructure (PKI), or any other simple or even exotic technologies. The

---

*Remarks made at the National High Performance Computing and Communications Council Meeting, "High End Computing in an Insecure World," Apr. 3, 2002. As reported in press reports including *Security Wire Digest*, April 8, 2002 and *Computerworld*, April 8, 2002.

Exhibit 1. Personal Information Security Plan

XXX Company

Personal Information Security Plan
Date:

Plan period: From: To:

Employee name: Location: Network user ID:

1. Home computer profile

    Computer make, type (If a laptop is used, describe the type of locking mechanism used.):

    Home ISP: AOL _____ WorldNet _____ MSN _____ Earthlink _____ Other _____

           Access type: Dial-up _____ DSL _____ Cable modem _____

           Number of times a week used for work:

    Home network (if applicable): Ethernet _____ Token Ring _____ Wireless _____

2. **Home protection profile** (Please describe methodologies or technology used at home to protect computers and networks.):

    Anti-virus software (vendor, version):

    Personal firewall (vendor, version):

    Other:

3. **Annual security plan goals** (List courses to be taken, preventive measures to be undertaken in the upcoming year. Include skills courses, awareness courses, and any continuing education classes that are applicable.):

I agree that this accurately represents my use of corporate computer resources. In addition, I have read and understand the corporate information security policies for my position.

_____   _____

Employee signature   Manager signature

This section to be completed by supervisor.

From annual security audit, describe any security violations or compliance issues:

Number of times passwords were manually reset:

Number of violations of Web access policies (if any):

Indicate any involvement of employee in audit points:

Changes in employee access profile or security clearance:

---

emphasis here is on the routine things an employee does that can create risk to the company.

The items to be measured include the need to track compliance at a technical level, however. It is not practical to rely solely on the employee writing a plan and taking a pledge of compliance. It is important that the technical approaches to compliance be used and the results be included in the evaluation of the effectiveness of the plan. These should not come as any surprise to a security professional and the tools should be part of the arsenal:

- *Password-cracking programs:* Measuring the strength of the passwords used by the employees
- *Log-in tracking reports:* Recording the number of times the user tried to log in remotely and succeeded or failed
- *Network security audits:* Tracking the use of dial-up lines or DSL access

All these tools produce data that would be sent to the employee's supervisor for use in the annual performance appraisal.

The idea here is to broaden the focus of information security policies in the mind of the employee. By making each individual employee accountable for making and executing a personal security plan, they have a stake in the process of practicing safe computing at their company. They also have to become more knowledgeable about the effect of their actions on the state of security as a whole.

How the Plan Would Work. Prior to the annual performance review, every employee would be required to complete a personal security plan. The plan would be designed in conjunction with the company's information security policies that would dictate key items such as remote access policies, password policies, and secure computing standards. The individual's plan would consist of his own usage profile plus written plans for the year to use corporate computing resources in compliance with the published information security policies.

For example, people who work from home using dial-up lines might be required to use a smart card or other two-factor authentication scheme as part of their access methodology. This may be combined with the use of a personal firewall and installation of anti-virus software. The employee would use this form to describe his remote access profile and how he is going to comply with corporatewide policies. Another aspect of the plan would be for the employee to sign a notice that he understands and complies with the corporate information security policy manual. This annual certification can become important if the employee ever is investigated for a violation.

Once this form is completed, the employee would give it to his supervisor for approval. The supervisor would be required to review the plan to ensure that it complies with corporate standards. Once approved, a copy of the plan is given back to the employee for his personal files and the original is kept on file with other vital employee records.

The plans would be useful to the Chief Information Security Officer to use to check for overall compliance at the department and division levels. The CISO would have the ability to review the plans from a corporatewide perspective, but the development and compliance at the individual level is left to the employee and his supervisor.

Enforcement of the Personal Security Plan. Enforcement of the plan would be similar to the managerial approach but much more focused and specific. All employees would have to have a plan, and the effectiveness of both individual plans and the process as a whole could be measured and managed. Employees would know that their job performance and compensation would now be linked to their plan. HRMS should be satisfied with this approach as they are not the enforcers of the plan, merely of the compliance mechanism. Audit likewise would be gratified with this approach as it is measurable and has clear lines of accountability that they too can measure. Finally, the IS professional should be the happiest of all as he has a way to bring the entire organization into the process of information security policy compliance and enforcement.

Each company using the approach is responsible for matching the results to any actions taken with respect to the employee's performance appraisal. The weight that the personal security plan carries for appraisal purposes will vary from company to company. In cases where there is a high-risk profile, the plan will logically carry more weight than in low-risk profile positions. Failure to complete the plan or failure to execute the plan then becomes the negative side of enforcement, requiring disciplinary action to be taken on the part of the responsible manager.

This alone will not end all risk to the company. Nor can it be a substitute for technical approaches to solving technology problems. What this can do is move the responsibility to the point closet to compliance, i.e., the actual employee required to comply with the policy.

Support for This Idea. Recently, the National Infrastructure Protection Counsel (NIPC) published some simple security tips that fit this strategy. Exhibit 2 shows the tips they recommend for small business and home computer users.

These tips could become the basis of any company's personal strategy to be used to educate employees about their responsibilities. They then become the core elements to be used in the creation of that company's version of a personal security plan.

Exhibit 2. Seven Simple Security Tips: Chart for Small Business and Home Computer Users[a]

1. *Use strong passwords.* Choose passwords that are difficult or impossible to guess. Give different passwords to all accounts.
2. *Make regular backups of critical data.* Backups must be made at least once each day. Larger organizations should perform a full backup weekly and incremental backup every day. At least once a month the backup media should be verified.
3. *Use virus protection software.* That means three things: (1) having it on your computer in the first place, (2) checking daily for new virus signature updates, and (3) actually scanning all the files on your computer periodically.
4. *Use a firewall as a gatekeeper between your computer and the Internet.* Firewalls are usually software products. They are essential for those who keep their computers online through the popular DSL and cable modem connections, but they are also valuable for those who dial in.
5. *Do not keep computers online when not in use.* Either shut them off or disconnect them from Internet connection.
6. *Do not open e-mail attachments from strangers.* Regardless of how enticing the subject line or attachment may be, be suspicious of any unexpected e-mail attachment from someone you know because it may have been sent without that person's knowledge from an infected machine.
7. *Keep your protection updated.* Regularly download security patches from your software vendors.

[a] Consult www.nipc.gov for more information.

These plans would need to be updated on an annual basis and the various items in the plan would be updated both as the employee's usage changes and as technology changes. But once the process is started, documenting the changes becomes a routine part of the employee's duties.

The Personal Security Plan: Phase 2

This program could be expanded in a second phase to take into account actual job performance-related criteria. The first phase concentrates on the employee's personal computer usage and extends to any offsite access of the company network. In the next phase, details are added about the employee's current usage of information and computers while at work. This phase would be more directly related to identity management initiatives that address role-based access and authentication.

The following elements could be added to the plan in this phase:

- Information access level and date of last change (public, confidential, private, secret)
- Authorization level (read, write, update)
- System-level access, if any (supervisor, operator, analyst)

Additional information could be added that would address other policy compliance issues such as development of additional skills and certifications as well as changes in access levels. For example, as an employee transitions from one role to another it is important to remove his old access credentials as soon as possible. Start and stop dates of access credentials should be added to the plan as well as results of audits of those credentials.

The security plan for the individual would then have all the components that describe the access rules, authorization levels, and records of compliance with those rules. This would be much more specific and would require more time on the part of the supervisor to review and assess. The supervisor would be required to review violations, audit logs, and document any violations that occurred during the planning period.

The advantage of this approach is that it would bring the employee full circle in his understanding of his role and rights for information access to his actual experience and performance. This is again aimed at getting individual accountability and making that the key element of the enforcement process.

This chapter has not addressed the issue of tying compliance to compensation. This is a good discussion topic and one that will be left for another time and place. In many companies today, compensation plans have been uncoupled from the performance appraisal process. Many firms are proponents of the "total compensation" concept that reports to the employee his salary, benefits, and bonuses. The employee's performance appraisal, which includes compliance with policies such as the one that would drive the personal security plan, is part of that overall process. Compensation is then linked to compliance along with other issues such as corporate performance. The amount and degree of the linkage between compliance and compensation is up to the individual firm.

Conclusion

The subtitle of this chapter is "Moving Toward a New Way of Enforcing Security Policy." In no way is this approach intended to be the end point of the journey to getting full enforcement of information security policy. This approach gives the security professional a practical way to move enforcement of security policy further along in the organization. It also moves enforcement from a top-down model to a bottom-up model and takes into account individual accountability for policy compliance.

By going beyond awareness and enlisting the assistance of other areas such as Human Resources, security policy becomes a routine part of the job rather than the exception. By making it routine and including it in the measurement of compliance with other, more traditional policies, it becomes more feasible to expect that the goal of compliance is achieved. After all, the goal is compliance and enforcement is only the mechanism.

Chapter 9
Authentication Models and Strategies

Introduction to Authentication

Most people in business, if asked about information security, think first about their own use of user IDs and passwords. Their view of the world of security is the narrow one of authentication systems and authorization schemes. They do not have a thorough understanding of all the other issues regarding information security and risk reduction. While this makes the protection of information a challenge, authentication systems do make a good point to opening the larger discussion of information security. It is also important to understand authentication and authorization in depth and to link those two concepts together to build a model of security that can be understood and shared by the information security professional and the business manager.

This starts with a definition of terms:

Authentication: A process of validating or verifying someone's identity. When this term is used with respect to information technology it can refer to an individual, a computer, or a resource.

Authorization: The rights or privileges that are granted to an authenticated entity.

There is a considerable amount of discussion that occurs in this simple model of authentication and authorization because this is the basis for the entire way security has been designed and built. The strengths and weaknesses of this model are that it is designed to let authenticated people and processes do authorized things while at the same time allowing unauthenticated people and processes to do nothing.

The challenge facing the security professional is to find a cost-effective and efficient way to verify identity with a minimum of errors. That has to be done in the face of multiple systems and applications, all of which may have diverse rules and architectures.

To understand this process requires some in-depth understanding of the concepts behind identity and the ways it can be verified. This has become a major part of the information security industry and has developed its own subculture, called identity management. Understanding these concepts starts with a more detailed look into authentication and authentication strategies.

Understanding authentication and authorization is an important concept for executive management in today's technology-dependent world. Sixty percent of U.S. businesses today say that they rely on information technology for daily business, according to research attributed to the Gartner Group.* That reliance means that firms have to trust their information and information provided to them by others. Trust in that sense can only be established if the identity of the business partner can be proven accurately. If you know with whom you are doing business, and you know they are who they say they are, then you have the basis for trust.

Understanding authentication of identity is then the key factor in a business relationship. There is a wealth of information available about authentication and authentication services. Much of that information is highly technical and assumes a high degree of understanding of the principles of authentication on the part of the reader. Most senior managers lack that depth of understanding and defer to their experts when the topic comes up. This chapter is intended to provide the executive and senior managers the information they need to understand these principles and how they apply to their business.

Authorization is a related topic that will not be explored in great depth in this discussion. Management of system resources and information and controlling their usage is part of another, though related, management decision process. Resource management is part of the responsibilities of information technology operations management. Controlling what authorized people and processes can do with information falls into the responsibilities of information owners (see Chapter 5) and their designated administrators. There are some related issues that interact with the management of identity and authentication systems. As mentioned, there is a concept of least privilege that is the core of authorization. The people within an organization who decide on authentication may or may not be the same ones making decisions on authorization. When it comes to information as an asset, at a high level the decision on authorization should be made by the owners of that information (see Chapter 5). Those owners can delegate the administration of their authorization scheme to others, a process known as delegation of authority.

---

*Adams, Tony, Investment Decisions: Preparing for Organizational Disasters, Gartner, January 29, 2003.

This chapter focuses on identity and the principles of verifying identity through the use of authentication tools and processes.

Authentication Defined

In the earliest days of computers, there were no systematic approaches to authenticating a user of the system. Early computers had physical input devices such as punch cards that helped limit access. Authorized users were those people who had physical access to the input and output devices. Their identity could be validated by conventional means: an ID badge, a photograph, or checking a name off a list.

As systems grew in complexity so did the need to verify who was using them and that they were performing functions that had been approved by the managing authority. This had two goals, the first of which was financial, ensuring that the computer was being used efficiently. Directly related to that was a desire to find a way to allocate the cost of the computer to areas that benefit from its use. The second goal was to find a way to limit the use of the computer to only those purposes that had been approved by management. That was also a financial goal as the computer was a scarce and costly resource and demand for usage far outstripped available computer time. Neither of these goals is directly related to those we associate today with information security. When system administrators implemented these financial protections, they also began the process of limiting access, meaning that they were taking the first step to protecting the same resources, which is an information security principle. As a result, a lot of the early security models came from accounting for computer resources. The idea of protecting those resources from abuse or misuse was secondary at best.

A related idea to keep in mind is that early computers were single-user, single-process systems. Only one program could run at a time. As computers became more powerful, that shifted rapidly to a multi-user, single-process system and then to the multi-user, multi-process computers that we know today. This has been an evolutionary process and it has occurred with several false steps along the way. To better understand how security has evolved, it is also necessary to learn more about how computers function.

That leads to having to define some other terms that are important to understanding authentication and authorization:

Trust: For this discussion, trust is a concept based on authentication. A user or process that has been properly authenticated can be trusted and therefore endowed with certain privileges.

Process: A process is a technical term that defines computer code functionality. For example, there is a read process and a write process.

Resource: Computers have a central processing unit (CPU) that performs control functions and accesses different resources such as memory and input/output devices.

The first step in implementing security is to create a list of users and require that all jobs submitted to run on the computer have an identifier. That would apply to processes that ran on the computer system whether they were an application (or "job" in the beginning) or whether they were a process that the computer needed to run the application. In this model, the computer itself is just another user. The term "superuser" is often used in this context. The computer must have the authority to run all processes to successfully execute the jobs that it was designed to run.

This leads immediately to the creation of a hierarchy of users and is related to the concept of trust. The superuser runs with the authority to execute any process while other users will have less authority and may only access information or run processes that are necessary for them to be successful. This is a concept known as "least privilege." There will be more on this idea later in the chapter.

Understanding these ideas is important as it sets the framework to understand why authentication is so important to the world of information security. If a user or process is authenticated, it obtains certain privileges and powers. It is then considered trusted and will not be asked further to prove its identity.

This then is the goal of the hacker — trying to access a system and gain authorization to execute or function as a "privileged" process. The hacker has many ways of attempting to gain access, but the goal is always the same. Therefore, the primary defense mechanism for security computers and information technology resources is to have a way to verify identity with a high degree of confidence. The related goal is to protect the administration of the identification process from misuse.

Authentication Choices

Authentication and access control mechanisms are almost synonyms in this context. Many books on security place the concept of authentication within the context of access control systems. Identification and authentication are two sides of the same coin. For every means of identifying a person or resource, there is a corresponding way to validate that identity. In doing so, there are some requirements that are common to any system of authentication: it should be easy to use, fast, difficult to break, and highly accurate. These requirements sometimes conflict with one another, and it is up to the person responsible for the authentication process to decide which features will have priority. For example, ease of use often conflicts with the degree of difficulty to break the system. A simple example is that a lock on a door can help restrict access to only those people who have a key. The underlying assumption is that all key holders are authentic and ownership of the key is proof of identity. That may be a reasonable idea if there are few keys and the owners protect the keys from being stolen or copied. This gets to be a risky proposition if the keys have been copied and there is no record of who owns a key.

This is directly addressed in the three factors of authentication, which are common to all systems and schemes:

1. *Something you know.* This is the basis of passwords. In the simplest sense, a password is a secret shared between two or more people. When the identity of one of those people is challenged, they use the password for validation. Passwords have their own set of strengths and weaknesses. The simpler the password, the easier it is to remember and the easier it is to break. Complex passwords are more resistant to being guessed, but they are more difficult to remember. People understand this trade-off and information security professionals are kept busy dealing with this conflict.
2. *Something you have.* This is a physical device used as a means of verifying identity. An ID badge with a picture of the owner is a common form of this factor. The key to this factor is that the "something you have" is trusted by its very existence; therefore, it needs to be difficult to copy or tamper with and it needs to be easy to use and carry.
3. *Something you are.* This is the realm of things like biometric identifiers. Common examples of this factor are fingerprint, hand geometry, retina pattern, and speech recognition. All of these are considered a "strong" means of identification because they are thought of as impossible to fake. There are a number of issues associated with this type of authentication that have led to it being not widely adopted. One of those issues is that the accuracy of the reader can be variable, which may introduce errors into the verification process. Another problem is the cost of the system and the degree of difficulty in using such a system. Yet another problem has to do with the error rate in identity checking.

There are two types of error with any of these methodologies. The first is a false acceptance rate (FAR). FAR is a function of the accuracy and speed of the system. Generally, the higher the rate of speed of verifying identity, the higher the error rate and the more often a false identity will be accepted. The other common error is the false reject rate (FRR). That is a measure of the number of times a person with the correct credentials is rejected by the system. The false acceptance rate is the one that deals with permitting access to the wrong person and has the higher degree of risk, while the false reject rate is more frustrating to the user as it prevents the correct people from doing their job. There are graphs that show these rates for different authentication products, and there is a point where the two types of error meet, called the crossover error rate (CER). The CER is seen as a comparative measure between the error rates and a means of comparison. Trying to manage around the error rates can be difficult as any error can be frustrating to the user and can create a vulnerability for the hacker to exploit. Maintaining a balance between those rates is part of the duties of the manager of the system. There are no perfect answers to this problem. Part of the question that should be asked by the executive management team has to do with their tolerance for either error.

Biometric authentication systems are often thought to be the most accurate and therefore the most desirable. Even biometric systems can be spoofed, which is to say fooled. Molds of fingerprints can be made and used to fool fingerprint scanners. There are some people who work in fields that lead to high error rates with fingerprint systems, such as bank tellers and stone workers. Digital pictures of a person's eye can be made and used to fool a retina scanner.

While none of these systems is foolproof or completely resistant to tampering, they are all considered to be more accurate than an ID-and-password-based system.

Often there will be a combination of factors used in an authentication system. Some systems require the person to carry an object with him (something he has) that is presented as part of the authentication process. That may be a card or other device that matches something on the validating side of the process, similar to a lock and key. The device may require a personal identification number (PIN) (something you know) in order for it to be activated and used. In some cases, the biometric identifier may be stored on such a device and used in conjunction with a PIN. The combination of a credential and PIN is known as two-factor authentication; the combination of a credential, PIN, and biometric identifier is called three-factor authentication.

In all cases, the same concepts apply to objects and people. Computers can be authenticated to each other using more than one authentication factor. One computer can present its credentials to another, perhaps in the form of a digital certificate. That certificate may be accompanied by a shared secret, a PIN, the value of which is known to both machines.

There is an additional approach to the "something you know" factor of authentication that has recently been gaining popularity. With the increasing use of relational databases, it has become possible to change the "something you know" from a simple user ID and PIN to what is called non-wallet information, making the challenge/response more interactive. Innovators like Choicepoint have decided to make use of the vast store of personal information in their databases and take a creative approach to the authentication challenge/response paradigm. For example, instead of a user ID and PIN, the system might ask for a user ID, user name, and the amount of the person's car payment, or their previous address. This is called nonwallet data as it is historical in nature and would not typically be found in the person's wallet. The information in the challenge can change with each access attempt, increasing the degree of difficulty for someone attempting to fraudulently access the system. With the growth in identity theft, this can be a powerful tool. Someone who steals wallet-type information out of a mailbox would be unaware of the more historical factors that the real person would know. The real person would answer the challenge correctly, but the imposter would be unable to correctly respond to the question. It remains to be seen if this will emerge as a standard tool in the authentication world, however.

Protecting credentials is another major function of authentication. In the physical world, credentials are issued by recognized authorities and kept in tamper-proof containers. This is the modern driver's license, which is issued by a government agency once the person has brought other proof of identity (birth certificate, etc.). Years ago, a driver's license might have been a printed form with information typed in. Today, most licenses are made of plastic and are embossed with holograms or other difficult-to-copy images. Most people accept them without question as a result.

The trust in the issuing authority is another feature of authentication systems. Both parties in an authentication process have to trust the credentials that they are using. For people, that may be a government agency as in the previous example of a driver's license. For computers, that may be a third-party authority that both computers have agreed to use. Use of a third party for trust creates a need to have an infrastructure similar to the role a government plays.

Public Key Infrastructure

One of the technologies for authentication that has been widely discussed, if not widely accepted, is pubic key infrastructure (PKI). PKI combines the ideas of multi-factor authentication with the idea of a trusted third party controlling the credentials. This is a fairly complex idea, but worth understanding as it has become a part of the lexicon of the information security world. The following explanation is a greatly simplified one, taking a few liberties in describing this complex process.

Understanding PKI requires a brief discussion of encryption and secrecy. Encrypting messages is an ancient means of ensuring the privacy of communications. The general techniques involved go back to Roman times. There are basically two forms of encryption: shared keys, also called secret keys, and public keys. In a secret-key system, two parties agree on an algorithm for encrypting their messages, and they use a key that is known to both of them to encrypt and decrypt their messages. The algorithm can be as simple as substituting one letter for another with the key being the offset (B for A is a one-letter offset, "1" is the key). More complex forms of this encryption have evolved over time with the most famous being the story of the German Enigma machine used during World War II. Today, there are a number of well-known encryption standards and algorithms using secret keys such as the DES (Data Encryption Standard) algorithm and PGP (Pretty Good Privacy).

Over time it has become obvious that, although these methods work well, their weakness is the shared key. If that key is compromised, then it is easy to decrypt the message and the system is useless. The way to help avoid that is to change the shared key, but the distribution of the key is another weak point. If only two people share the secret key, changing it is a straightforward and simple process. If many people or devices rely on the same key, the problem of changing that key and protecting it while the change is occurring becomes very difficult. Secret key systems are in wide use in the commercial and military marketplaces. They work very well and are ideal for protecting the secrecy of a message. Systems like this also are good for protecting high volumes of messages as well as for protecting large messages. As stated, though, the weak spot is in protecting the shared key. The other weakness comes from the increases in computer speed and power in the marketplace today. Trying to decrypt a message without having access to the shared key is called a brute-force attack and these once took months or years to do. Today, with the ability to link large numbers of high-speed computers together, a single message can be broken in a matter of weeks, if not days, just by guesswork.

A way around the problem of key management and a shared secret key is a public key system. A public key system uses advanced mathematical techniques to create a process where two or more parties have access to a public key although they can select and maintain their own secret key. In a sense, this is like an advanced version of a user-ID-and-PIN pair. In a public key system, it is the combination of a private key and a public key that encrypts the message, and a different private key and the shared public key can be used to decrypt the message. The mathematical formulas used make this combination almost impossible to break. The use of a private/public key pair is also thought of as a way to authenticate a user with greater certainty than with a secret key alone. The mathematics involved in creating the full key usually involves not only the private key of the sender and the shared secret key; it also includes a time stamp and a hash total. The combination of the time stamp and the hash means that the receiver can be assured that the sender is the one and only person who is capable of sending the message that was received.

The mathematics involved in PKI has been tested and validated a number of times. This process has been proven successful and is in wide acceptance around the world. It does come with a high cost, as there is a large infrastructure (the "I" in PKI) that is built around it. The infrastructure costs are usually shared by the many people who use the system. This type of system works well where proof of identity is as important as protecting the contents of the message itself. Unfortunately, the cost of developing and administering such a system is also the reason that it has not gained wider acceptance in the marketplace. There are other benefits of PKI, one of which is that it is much more difficult to break a PKI-encrypted message using a brute-force attack than it is to break a secret key message.

Some vendors have begun to market their PKI-based products as an authentication system. This stretches the idea of authentication to some degree. PKI can be used to verify identity of a message sender, but it is not necessarily the best way to verify identity in the traditional computer user access control concept. That is because in the traditional sense the authentication that is being done is to grant someone access to a service or process after which their identity is unquestioned and the messages that are sent do not necessarily need to be kept secret. Secrecy is not free; when an encryption algorithm is used it requires additional computer resources for handling the message. Those resources have a cost in the time it takes to translate the message text from its encrypted format to clear text that can be used by people or systems. PKI as a tool for authentication adds to the system resource utilization rate. The benefits of such a system, as with all applications, must be reviewed by management in terms of its cost.

Digital signatures are related to PKI on a conceptual level. There is the Digital Signature Standard (DSS), published by the National Institute of Standards and Technology (NIST). Digital signatures are used as a means of message authentication rather than a means of personal authentication. Like PKI, it uses public and private key pairs for encrypting the message. Yet another related technology is digital certificates. This is a common form of protecting communications using public and private keys. Again, the most common usage is for message protection and not for individual user authentication. The difference to some people in this discussion is very subtle. For a security professional, these differences are significant and are core issues in choosing the right technology for the right application. The senior executive should be aware of the technologies and understand that the major decisions are over issues such as threats, risks, and the cost of mitigating those threats and risks. Understanding these different technologies at a detailed level is a role best left to the organization's security team and its management.

This makes a good point to discuss the operational issues associated with authentication systems and business plans and operations.

Administration and Authentication: Management Issues

Understanding the technical underpinnings of authentication models is the first step in the process of dealing with the management issues they pose to a business. There are some underlying assumptions that should be revisited at this point.

As stated at the outset of this chapter, when policies are established for a company, one of the core information security policies is that information is an asset, and access to information will be permitted on a least-privilege basis. That then implies the need to have access control processes as part of the IT management scheme. A second policy has to do with having control decisions based on risk management — the controls that are to be used should be commensurate with the risks facing a business. This is all very straightforward, as it means that in a high-risk business there needs to be controls that match those risks. Likewise, the value of the assets to be protected must also be part of this equation.

Translating this into everyday usage, this means that management has a responsibility to have a cost-effective control system in place that addresses the risks peculiar to the business. It is not reasonable to protect $1 of assets with $1 million in controls, and the reverse is also true. When dealing with authentication models and strategies, this is the place to start as opposed to starting by looking at alternatives of encryption algorithms.

A list of questions that senior management should ask in this process includes:

1. What is our risk exposure (high, medium, low)?
2. What is our risk tolerance (high, medium, low)?
3. Do we have a centralized organization, or a decentralized one?
4. Can we dictate our technology choices to our business partners and customers, or do we have to comply with industry standards and norms?
5. What are our goals with respect to speed of processing vs. security (in general, there is an inverse relationship between throughput and security)?

These questions can best be summarized as "how much security can we afford?" There is a direct relationship between overhead from administration and cost. Chapter 10 discusses the subject of single sign-on.

There are two major technical points to consider that are part of these questions. One is the decision regarding a centralized or decentralized administrative model, and the second deals with the ease-of-use issues.

Almost all security systems can be administered either from a single point or through the use of one of several decentralized models. The choice is more a management one than a technical one. The bulk of security administrative activities involve the enrollment process — adding, updating, and deleting records. Security administrators can designate local people to handle these tasks without compromising the integrity of the system. One of the other routine functions, password changes and password resets, can be automated. The fear in using a decentralized model is that the remote administrators will not use the same level of care that a centralized staff would use in the same situation. To most executives, this issue applies to a wide variety of job functions and roles, but to a security administrator this is a security management rather than a risk management issue and as such is part of his responsibility. Choosing between a centralized and decentralized administrative model is a decision that should be looked at from an organizational perspective rather than a technical one. There are control issues in either case that will have to be addressed, such as the change management process and the monitoring of certain sensitive positions. There are also training and auditing issues that need to be resolved and are beyond the authority of most security administrators. Each of these tasks must be done in either case, so any one of them should not be the deciding issue in this decision.

The other major point in this decision has to do with ease of use. This has several contexts: ease of adding and deleting records, ease of sign-on, and type of identification credentials to be used. Understanding password management issues and developing a better strategy for managing passwords is an important part of this process. Password management issues are largely technical in nature, with the basic notion that the longer the password the better, as well as the more complex the password the better. What is important for this discussion is that management is aware of these issues and included in the discussion. There are many related management issues in both the ease-of-use discussion and the administrative model, and these issues should have more than just the support of executive management; they should have their involvement in the decision-making process.

Overhead in security administration adds to the cost of the effort. There are costs to purchase a system, implementation costs and administrative ones. As discussed previously, the decisions that are made in this area are complex ones and the greater the security desired, the higher the costs associated with achieving that goal. There are ways to address the issue of overhead associated with security administration, but it too comes with its own set of costs.

There are also a number of risks that need to be discussed with each model. The goal of a security system is to provide effective protection to

Exhibit 1. Identity Theft Chart

Identity theft is a growing crime that is getting a lot of attention from the public and law enforcement agencies. With the advent of the Department of Homeland Security, this focus will grow more in the future. Protection of identity and the credentials that authenticate a person's identity is important to executives as a business issue as well as in their personal lives.

The short definition of identity theft is the act of misappropriating information, documents, or other materials that are personal in nature and used to define someone's identity. This includes forgery of documents or alteration of them for a criminal purpose. In 2000, a study by the Privacy Rights Clearinghouse showed that it cost individuals, on the average, 175 hours to resolve identity theft problems.[a] This is a serious issue for businesses as they are both a source of information on identity and a user of such information. Businesses that collect information on customers and employees must be aware of the exposure they have to potential misuse of that information and should be taking appropriate risk mitigations steps, including:

- Protecting any credentials issued by that business that are used to define a person's identity. This includes access control badges, ID cards, and other forms of identification. Any credentials issued should be difficult to tamper or modify by unauthorized personnel.

- Privacy protection is part of the effort to protect identity. Protecting privacy is much more than issuing disclosure statements. It includes verifying sources of information to ensure they are legitimate as well as limiting uses of personal information only for legitimate purposes.

- Protection of resources and infrastructure from unauthorized access is critical. If a company validates identity electronically through the use of digital certificates of advanced identity management schemes such as PKI, that company must take the appropriate steps to protect servers, networks, and other parts of its infrastructure. Using the most advanced methods of verifying identity will be invalidated if the sources of that information are not protected properly.

Businesses today have a fiduciary responsibility to aid in the fight against identity theft. It is not possible for a firm to opt out of this battle because it is as reliant as the consumer on proof of identity.

---

[a] www.stopidentitytheft.org.

---

assets and resources. The type of system chosen should address the risks inherent to business. The security system should not inadvertently add to those risks.

Identity Theft

No discussion of authentication today would be complete without mentioning identity theft (see Exhibit 1). This is a growing problem that is getting an increasing amount of attention from a number of sources.

Authentication schemes are part of the fight to protect and manage identity. Whichever methodology is chosen to authenticate an individual or resource, the executive management team must understand and appreciate the importance of protecting the system itself from misuse. That means that authentication systems are part of the critical infrastructure of a business and as such should receive the highest level of protection. Losing control of the authentication system poses greater risk than losing control of the information assets of the business itself. Without a means to ensure the accuracy of the authentication system there is no way to restrict the access to information and to protect it from intentional or inadvertent misuse.

This is also a problem for executives as consumers and as individuals. Loss of their own identity credentials poses a personal risk and a risk to the business. Executives should be taking the lead in their company in educating people in the need to protect their own credentials and personal information. Exhibit 2 is a checklist from the state of Georgia's Web site on identity theft, www.stopidentitytheft.org. There are numerous other places to go for information on this issue, and they should be part of the regular awareness training given to staff.

There are other threats and risks involved in the authentication management process and these too need the attention of senior management.

Risks and Threats Associated with Authentication Schemes

No discussion on authentication would be complete without looking at the risks and threats directly associated with identity management. This is an area that receives a lot of attention in security literature as it is core to understanding the benefits of the different authentication systems.

When looking at the risks associated with authentication, the central idea is to keep the bad guys out and let the good guys do only what they are authorized to do. The issue of dealing with unauthorized access is the one that most people are familiar with, and looking at it in greater depth will help identify the key strategic management issues associated with authentication.

There are two major threats to consider that authentication addresses. The first threat is unauthorized access. There are two common methods of attack by an intruder, the first of which is social engineering. Social engineering is the process of obtaining false credentials through pretending to be an authorized person. This can be as simple as showing up at the door and claiming to have forgotten an employee access card. The intruder usually has done his homework and has obtained a valid name from a telephone directory or a Web site. Using that information he may guess a user ID and ask to have a new password issued, claiming to have "forgotten" his.

Exhibit 2. Identity Theft Victim's Checklist

If you are an identity theft victim, take the following steps:

1. Contact each of the three major credit reporting agencies and request that a fraud alert be placed in your credit file.

   - Equifax, P.O. Box 740250, Atlanta, Georgia 30374-0250, (800) 525-6285 or www.equifax.com
   - Experian, P.O. Box 1017, Allen, Texas 75013, (888) 397-3742 or www.experian.com
   - TransUnion, P.O. Box 6790, Fullerton, California 92634, (800) 680-7289 or www.transunion.com

2. Contact companies that provided credit or anything else of value to the thief who stole your identity.

   - Immediately call the companies, banks, etc., that have extended credit in your name.
   - After you contact the police and Governor's Office of Consumer Affairs, follow up with a letter to the credit companies explaining that you did not make the charges on your statement or that you never requested new credit that was issued through fraudulent use of your identity.
   - Include in the letter all factual information such as statements or other documents that back you up.
   - Include a copy of your police report and a fraud affidavit.

3. Contact your local police or sheriff's department and make a report. Be sure to record the report number.

   - Explain how your identity was stolen.
   - Provide them with copies of statements or other documents that support your case.

4. Contact the Georgia Office of Consumer Affairs (OCA), the Federal Trade Commission (FTC), and the Internet Fraud Complaint Center (IFCC) to report the theft of your identity. The FTC is the national clearinghouse for identity theft information.

   - Contact OCA at (404) 651-8600 or (800) 869-1123 or www.ganet.org/gaoca.
   - Contact FTC at (877) ID-THEFT or www.consumer.gov/idtheft.
   - Contact IFCC at www.ifccfbi.gov.

5. At the FTC Web site or at the Equifax Web site, download the universal fraud affidavit, fill it out, and submit it to applicable creditors.

   - FTC: www.consumer.gov/idtheft.
   - Equifax: www.equifax.com.

6. After making telephone contact with the credit reporting agencies, follow up with a letter.

   - Explain that someone has stolen your identity and what actions the thief has taken.

(continued)

Exhibit 2. Identity Theft Victim's Checklist (Continued)

- Give factual information, including copies of statements, documents, and police reports that back you up.
- Request that a fraud alert be placed in your credit file.
- State that credit should not be granted unless you or your spouse is contacted for verification.

7. Depending on the nature of the fraud, you may want to contact the following organizations in addition to those listed above:

- Social Security Administration: If your Social Security number has been used in an unauthorized manner, call the Fraud Hotline at (800) 269-0721 or access the Web site: www.ssa.gov.
- Georgia Department of Motor Vehicles: If a motor vehicle is involved, call (404) 362-6002 or access the Web site: www.dmvs.ga.gov.
- Local Post Office and U.S. Postal Inspection Service: If mail or a change of address is involved, access the Web site: http://www.usps.gov/Websites/depart/inspect/fraud/IdentityTheft.htm.
- Federal Bureau of Investigation: If fraudulent activity extends across state lines: www.fbi.gov/contact/fo/territory.htm.
- U.S. Secret Service: If counterfeit checks are involved, call (404) 331-6111 or access the Web site: www.ustreas.gov/usss/.
- U.S. Department of State: For lost or stolen passport: www.state.gov.
- Internal Revenue Service or Georgia Department of Revenue: If fraudulent tax returns are involved, access the Web sites: www.irs.gov or www2.state.ga.us/departments/DOR.

Source: www.stopidentitytheft.org.

Through the years this approach has been consistently successful and it does not matter if the security administration is centralized or decentralized; the risk is the same. Other methods include a brute-force attack where the intruder tries to guess a password of a valid user.

Another method is called spoofing, where a program is used in a manner similar to social engineering. The program is sent to a target system acting in an authorized manner (such as an e-mail attachment), but instead of executing a normal process, the program gathers information to aid the attacker. There are many other programmatic ways to gain access to a computer system or network. The basic concept behind "buffer overflow" attacks is to send a program that causes the operating system or some other program to fail, leaving in its place the intruder's program. This is actually a form of identity theft in that the unauthorized program is running in the place of the authorized one, hoping that the system will not notice the difference. In this case, the malicious code is trying to assume the identity of another program.

Each of the previous examples works in a similar manner. They rely on the existence and use of real credentials by an unauthorized person or program to work. The basic controls that have been discussed earlier such as password rules, audit alarms, and reports are aimed at reducing the risks posed by these threats. Different authentication systems address these risks in only slightly different ways. The most important thing for executives to understand is that these are real risks to their business that must be addressed; how they are addressed is of less importance.

There are other threats posed to authentication systems that can be very highly technical in nature. For example, wireless networks, if not properly configured, can provide an opening for a hacker to enter the corporate network without authorization. Even hardwired networks can be tapped and messages copied and modified if the proper system controls are not in place. This leads to the final discussion point around authentication: the remaining strategic management issues.

Other Strategic Issues Regarding Authentication Systems

There are three remaining categories to discuss regarding strategic issues around authentication systems: (1) interoperability, (2) staff enrollment (provisioning), and (3) auditing. Auditing has been briefly mentioned and it needs to be said again that authentication systems are part of the general control systems in IT infrastructure (see Chapter 14). As such, there needs to be in place controls that include management reviews of any alerts, alarms, and audit reports coming out of such a system. All authentication systems include those reports and controls, and it is management's duty to ensure that there is a follow-up process.

The staff enrollment/de-enrollment issue has also been mentioned in several places. This falls into the category of "there's no free lunch." Even the most modern and newest authentication systems have to have some way to add, update, and delete records. Some rely on Internet-based tools; others try an interface to the Human Resources system to speed the process of enrollment and add another level of control. The issue of guest users, remote users, and home-based employees should be included in the authentication system standards and policies. These issues are not different than any others but can be overlooked as organizations downsize and outsource various functions. Speed and accuracy are critical issues when looking at these risks. When an employee leaves the company, there is a window of time where he may still have valid access credentials, which can create tremendous risk to the firm. In some ways, speed is more important in removing a person from a system than in adding him. In any case, the costs and responsibilities for provisioning should be identified up front as part of an authentication project, and they should be tracked as any other operational cost.

The area of interoperability is perhaps the most complex of these issues and the one for which there are no simple answers. From the executive management perspective the key is to raise this issue and make sure that the answer fits in with the rest of the corporate IT strategy and infrastructure. The best security system in the world will not afford complete protection from threats if it is not maintained and monitored. Support in this case means committing resources to the full life cycle of the activity, not just to the initial installation.

Conclusion

Authentication is the basis for a secure system and for reducing risk. Managing, maintaining, and monitoring access rules and authorizations are core responsibilities for successfully protecting the IT and information assets of a business. Executive management needs to be a knowledgeable and willing partner in this process, and understanding the issues and helping guide the process will ensure that this is done in a practical manner.

Section III
Information Security Principles and Practices

Information security offers a wide variety of solutions to protecting information and information assets. There are some basic principles behind the development of a sound information security plan, and this section covers some of those basic principles in detail. It is not important for the senior executive to become an expert in this field; after all, that is the role of the information security professional. It is important that senior management become familiar with some of the terms and the underlying principles that drive the decisions it will be asked to make regarding the business and its commitment to security and privacy.

Chapter 10
Single Sign-On Security

Overview

In developing a strategic security program, there is always the need to balance productivity with security. In the effort to improve security, companies have evolved from the simple user ID and password system to the more sophisticated model of identity management. Identity management itself has become almost synonymous with single sign-on (SSO), the goal of which is to balance verification of identity with improved productivity. Identity management covers a broad area in the information security industry, including remote access, authentication schemes, password management, and user profile provisioning. Each of these areas is important in the creation of a comprehensive information security program. Single sign-on remains an important topic, worthy of an in-depth review and separate discussion.

As defined here, single sign-on means a comprehensive way of assisting people in accessing systems, networks, and business applications through reducing the number of times they need to prove their identity. This broad definition covers a variety of methodologies and systems that are available in the marketplace today. It includes certificate-based and directory-based systems as well as password and user ID synchronization.

Much has been written about single sign-on as a topic for more than a decade. Information security professionals have discussed single sign-on at length and yet it continues to be of interest to them and other information technology professionals. This chapter explores single sign-on from a strategic perspective, discussing the alternatives and the pros and cons of using it in the corporate world. The idea of considering this from a strategic viewpoint is important as it allows the security professional and the business manager to look at the broader issues of identity management while focusing on the key issues of user authentication and authorization that underlay the problems SSO attempts to address.

The Authentication Dilemma

In the early years of the information security profession, the initial goals were to control access to scarce computer resources and to protect computer systems from misuse. To accomplish this goal, various systems were devised to identify users of such systems and restrict what they could do once they had been granted access to the system or resource. These early access control systems fell into two major categories based on competing views of the problem. One scheme was to grant the user the rights to do everything except for a list of restricted activities. The other approach was to deny the user to do anything and then add permissions based on needs. Both approaches required a user to have an ID and password, although in many cases these were shared among several people. Another feature of these systems was that they were based on the idea that the user, once authenticated, was not challenged again to prove his identity.

Over time in business, more and more applications were added to computer systems and access to applications was restricted to identified users. This meant that a user might be asked to prove his identity again and again on a per-application basis. The user would sign on once to a resource and then would be asked to sign on again to an individual application. As more and more applications were added to a system, a user had to maintain an increasing number of user IDs and passwords to prove his identity.

In the academic and scientific community, a related problem arose as users wanted to gain access to more than one system to gather data or exchange information. Similar to the problem facing the business community, the scientific and academic community was being forced to maintain lists of approved users, and those users were being required to sign on to an ever-increasing number of systems. In the academic community, this challenged the normal view that information was a shared resource and that it should be accessible to anyone. The open exchange of information is one of the core values of academics; a computer system that limited access was frustrating at best.

Thus it became more and more burdensome to perform a job in both the business and academic worlds, and users began to complain about the difficulty of accessing and using systems. Each system had a separate database of user IDs and passwords. Systems had independent administrative tools as well, causing the people charged with protecting those systems also to have to sign on to multiple systems to perform administrative tasks. There were no industry standards for user ID length or password management. Some systems allowed the user's name to be used; others were limited to 8-bit alphanumeric IDs. Passwords too were not standardized by length or content; some systems required passwords with a minimum length, while others could be customized and adapted to use different password lengths. As the number of systems and authentication schemes grew, the problem of user authentication became more complex. People began to study the problem of authentication as more than a security issue; they began to look at it as a business issue that affected productivity and user satisfaction.

This research began to focus on how authentication is done in general, not just with computers. People are accustomed to having their identity verified in the course of their normal activities. Several authentication models were defined and these were used to see how the process could be improved.

It is also important here to describe the idea of one-to-one vs. one-to-many authentication. In the simplest implementation of authentication, we are describing a one-to-one relationship. A user requests access to a single system or application through the presentation and validation of his credentials; he is then granted access to perform whatever functions are appropriate for his job. This is like a key that will unlock only the one door that is fitted with the matching lock. If the user goes to another door, he will need yet another key.

In a one-to-many system, which is the basis of the concept of single sign-on, the user again presents his credentials for authentication and once that occurs he is given access to all systems or applications that are protected by that authentication system. This is analogous to having a master key to a large building: the key will let you into the building and it will give access to all areas within. To get into any particular office, you would not need to use that or any other key or request access from a receptionist or guard. The single key grants access to the entire facility.

The ideas behind authentication and authorization form the basic components of the information security practitioner's world. This is discussed in greater detail in Chapter 9. For the purpose of this discussion, the important concepts to remember about authentication and authorization are:

- Permit authorized people access to do their job.
- Restrict people to the minimum access necessary to perform their job.
- Prevent unauthorized people from doing anything.

This means, on the one hand, the goals are exclusion and restriction, limiting what a person can do. On the other hand, the goals of business require efficiency, and that means people must have access to all resources needed for them to be productive.

Security professionals were among the first to see the problem that these systems posed to business. They had to learn multiple administrative tools as different systems and technologies were added, as each vendor seemed to approach the problem differently. Most computer systems came with a native security system that had limited functionality, and they were not aimed at dealing with large user populations.

As these systems multiplied, so did the need to protect them with tools that allowed more granular controls than the generalized security systems offered. Add-on systems were developed that allowed for improved security administration, but they were not standard across vendors or operating systems. They did help with some of the problems, but they did not offer much help in reducing the number of times users were challenged to prove their identity.

Users perceived this as a problem and began to find ways around it. One of the most common solutions was to use the same ID name on multiple platforms. Users also tried to use simple passwords that were easy to remember and easy to maintain. The most common passwords in use are words such as "user" or "guest," neither of which do much to ensure the protection of the system or application. The goals of restricting access and protecting resources were conflicting with the ideals of use and productivity.

It seemed to the user community that security professionals were countering these growing problems by adding to them. Protocols were added to authentication systems that would require passwords to be changed on a prescribed basis, such as every 30 days. Auditing systems were also enlisted in the effort to ensure that users used hard-to-guess passwords. This only added to the users' perception of the problem as they now had to deal with multiple passwords expiring on different days on different systems. Instead of improving security, all this effort created the perception that security was the problem and not the solution.

The complaints were addressed to the people trying to protect those systems; they were asked to find a way to simplify the problem. The search for an SSO system was born.

The Many Definitions of Single Sign-On

One of the reasons that single sign-on receives so much attention is that the topic covers a wide area in the information security arena. When someone mentions single sign-on, he can be talking about authentication methodologies, authorization schemes, password synchronization, or one of several other areas of interest. There does not appear to be a firm consensus about the definition of single sign-on even among the many vendors of products that sell in this marketplace.

A goal in creating such a platform was to relieve the end user of the burden of remembering multiple passwords and user IDs. By creating one place for a user to sign on, there would be additional benefits for the security administrator:

- Reduced administrative overhead from having fewer user directories
- Improved security through having better control over user enrollment, including adding and deleting of user credentials
- Fewer errors from users attempting to sign on to systems for which they lack authorization

The most common definition of single sign-on is that it is a methodology that permits an authorized user to sign on to gain access to multiple systems or applications through a single process. Thus a user would be challenged once for access credentials and then authorized to use all the resources that he needs.

That one sentence says a lot about how difficult this has been over the years. For example, authenticating a user has become one of the cornerstones of the SSO industry. Once authentication is completed, there are many other technologies involved in enabling the user to execute job-related programs. Thus, what seems like a simple discussion of single sign-on can degenerate into arguments over authentication techniques and authorization schemes.

Keyword definitions used with single sign-on include:

- *Authentication:* Methodology used to determine that the person or object is actually who he/it claims to be
- *Authorization:* Granting or permitting an authorized user to perform a function

Within the realm of single sign-on there developed two major and somewhat competing approaches to solve this problem. The first approach looked at the problem from the viewpoint of a user trying to gain access to a system or server. This approach was first described in detail with the creation of the Kerberos project at MIT. This approach can best be thought of as dealing with the problem as one of authentication. If a user is properly authenticated, then he should not have to present his credentials a second time to prove his identity. If the system accepts the credentials as being valid, then the only thing left to do is to ensure that the credentials are valid and have not been compromised. After that, the problem becomes a simple one of granting access.

It is not surprising that MIT proposed a solution to this view of the problem as this is more of a scientific or academic view of access. This view focuses on object (networks, servers, systems, etc.) rather than applications (which here refers to a business-centric definition of application: payroll, for example). In the academic or scientific community, the access may be short lived and may not be repeated on a regular basis. Thus, granting someone access is the issue as opposed to authorizing them to do something once they have access.

The second approach takes more of an application view and deals more with the authorization side of the problem. This approach views the problem as more of an administrative issue and tries to solve it through reducing the costs associated with authorization. For example, in a large company a single user may need to access one system for general ledger data; a different system for his own personnel information; and multiple other systems, servers, or applications to perform his job functions. In this view of the world, the problem is one of efficiency. Users having to present their credentials to repeatedly prove their identity will often look for the path of least resistance and find a way to avoid the authentication challenge. They will use simple user IDs and passwords that are easy to remember and therefore easy for someone else to guess and abuse.

Given these two different views of the problem, it should not come as a surprise that several different solutions have been offered. The MIT Kerberos project is an authentication-based concept that has been copied and modified by others. Another approach has been to focus on the productivity issue. This approach starts with the concept of not trying to change the underlying authentication schemes on the disparate systems that are in use today. Instead, it focuses on bringing all those systems together into a single directory, where the user would only need to prove his identity once, and it would control his access to all other systems.

Several companies came forward with similar solutions based on using a single directory with user credentials. In all cases this approach leaves the underlying security application intact and gives the user a single entry point to multiple systems or business applications. This has proven to be a more popular approach than the ticket-based system. Typically, this approach involves the use of a directory (LDAP, Lightweight Directory Access Protocol, is the most popular protocol) that stores information about the security requirements of other systems. The user signs on to the directory system and, once authenticated, is then authorized to immediately use all systems for which he has been previously registered. This simplifies the user role while making the administrative role more complex. The security administrator must identify all applications and systems that will use the single sign-on directory, enroll all users into that directory, and maintain those relationships.

Although the directory-based approach offers improved productivity to the user through reducing the number of times he is challenged to prove his identity, it has a cost. That cost is the administrative effort it takes to implement such a system. The administrators must find all occurrences of an identity and load them into the directory for the system to work. If one system is missed, the user will have to sign onto that system in addition to the single sign-on directory.

This approach appears to be more of a business-centric view of the problem. Here users are more interchangeable parts of the problem, and they need to quickly be authenticated to perform specific and often narrow functions. In the simple sense of this view, a clerk needs access to an application so he can do his job. The actual access rules do not change much on a day-to-day basis.

Developing practical systems for single sign-on has proved to be an elusive goal that presents multiple challenges to the information security practitioner. While security professionals saw some benefits from simplifying the access control administration, they became aware of new risks associated with such systems.

Risks Associated with Single Sign-On

Information security professionals recognized that single sign-on also created a new element of risk. The major fear was that if the user's credentials were stolen, spoofed, or otherwise compromised, then the hacker would be given the "keys to the kingdom." Break into one system and you have broken into all of them. This fear led to many security professionals to oppose the use of SSO methodologies. By keeping authentication schemes separate, the idea was that a hacker or otherwise unauthorized user would be repeatedly challenged to prove either his identity or his need to know information in the system.

Another risk with single sign-on had to do with the solutions offered and concerns about availability. Using a Kerberos-style, ticket-based system meant that all access requests went through a single point of failure, the ticket-granting server. If this system went down or was compromised, then users would not be granted access even though their local servers or system resources were otherwise available. The immediate solution was to build redundancy into the design of SSO systems, thereby increasing the cost.

These two major issues led to a slow adoption rate for the available SSO solutions. Security professionals remained skeptical about the systems; users had the opposite view and pushed hard to reduce the degree of difficulty for accessing information.

Single Sign-On Alternative: A More In-Depth Review

To fully understand the concerns of the security professional it is necessary to review the major alternatives in greater depth. Each approach has its benefits and its supporters. There are also weaknesses with each approach as they look at the problem from slightly different perspectives.

Ticket-Based Single Sign-On Systems

As mentioned earlier, the best known of these type systems is Kerberos, developed at MIT in the mid-1980s. This system was designed to ease the problem of people accessing multiple systems remotely. It also lends itself to access that is information based as opposed to transaction based. This will become clearer as the system is explained.

The major concepts of a Kerberos-type SSO system are based on two ideas: strong authentication and encryption. In this view of the world, it is important that the user receives credentials that cannot be copied or modified as his credentials become the user's passport to navigate the many systems that are protected by this system. In reading about Kerberos, it is not as important to understand how all the encryption methodologies work as it is to understand how a single set of user credentials can be used to access multiple systems. The actual details of a system such as this are discussed more fully in Chapter 9. For the purposes of this discussion, we will use a very simplified version of what happens with a SSO system such as Kerberos. The major components of a Kerberos-style system are:

- A Kerberos client application that prompts the user to begin the authentication process. The user (or "subject" in Kerberos) enters a username and password. This information is forwarded to a Key Distribution Center (KDC) using a form of public key encryption.
- The KDC uses an Authentication Service (AS) to verify that the user/subject exists in the database. A new service is invoked, the Ticket Granting Service (TGS), that generates an encrypted session key with the user credentials as well as a Ticket Granting Ticket (TGT), which is also encrypted.
- The client application decrypts the TGS session key and deletes the password that was temporarily stored at the beginning of this process. The TGT is then a critical part of the session secret key.
- When the user/subject requests access to a protected system (or "object" in Kerberos), a message is sent to the TGS using the name of the object, the TGT, and a separate message containing the client ID and a time stamp, all of which is encrypted.
- The TGS then uses all that information to create a time-stamped ticket that is sent back to the client.
- The client can then use that ticket to directly communicate with the object.

As mentioned earlier, this approach makes sense when the number of objects, clients, and tickets generated are easy to measure and manage. This does create very strong user authentication and the user credentials are time-stamped and usable for only a predefined period of time.

There are other systems that have been developed using approaches similar to Kerberos, including KryptoKnight by IBM and SESAME (Secure

European Systems and Applications in a Multi-Vendor Environment), which was developed by the European Computer Manufacturers Association (ECMA).

Although the details of these systems differ, it is better to remember that they work conceptually the same way in that they create a session ticket that has a time stamp for further protection. The session ticket is the key to how these systems work. The object server or application validates the session ticket without requiring the user to sign onto the system directly; therefore, a user needs only to present his credentials once to generate a session ticket that then gives him access to all systems and resources that are protected by the system. The time stamp on the credential may be for minutes, hours, or days. The longer the time stamp is valid, the fewer times the user is challenged to reauthenticate.

Although these systems have been available for almost 20 years, they have not been widely adopted. They are seen as complex solutions requiring additional overhead to maintain. In the view of many security professionals, this offsets the goal of reducing the overhead associated with maintaining multiple authentication systems.

Directory-Based Single Sign-On Systems

The other major choice in an SSO application is the directory-based solutions discussed earlier in this chapter. In the directory-based approach, there is a single authentication server that is created with all users registered on that server; also on that server is a database containing all the other applications, servers, and systems that will accept the credentials from the authentication server. In a simplified view, these systems work as follows:

- The security administrator populates the database with all valid user names and target systems. Each user, once authenticated, is then identified as having rights to access one of the target systems.
- The authentication server is then authorized by the target systems to pass along the user information, becoming the *de facto* decision maker on who is or is not a valid user.
- The end user signs on to the authentication server using either a user ID/password combination or some stronger form of authentication such as a smart card.
- Once the user has been authenticated, his credentials are presented to the target system as valid and the authentication server is no longer part of the process. The user can request more than one system at a time. If access to additional systems or resources is needed, he goes back to the authentication server and starts the process over.

In this approach, the user is authenticated once and only once. The connection between the authentication server and the target systems is also protected. No one should be allowed to directly access the target system. Examples of this type approach have been developed by Netegrity, OBLIX, and IBM. All work in similar ways and are based on a directory that contains all the critical access information. Protecting the directory, of course, becomes critical to the security of such systems.

User Provisioning

When all SSO systems are reviewed, most people concentrate on looking at the system functionality, cost of acquisition, resource utilization, and ease of use. One area that tends to get overlooked is the effort it takes to populate the system with user credentials, system or object information, and the ongoing effort of adding, deleting, and updating that information. This effort is called user provisioning.

In the example of a directory-based system, for such a system to have maximum benefit the following information must be transferred to the directory database:

- *User names.* This can be very time-consuming as users may be enrolled different ways on different systems. John Smith, SSN #111-22-3333 may be listed as John Smith, JSmith, Smith, and 111-22-3333. The SSO administrator must find all occurrences of John Smith's username and register them for the system to be able to sign him once he is authenticated.
- *System credentials.* Systems or applications require that credentials are presented in a certain format. For example, John Smith may be the user ID on one system, with a "1" by the name indicating that it has been properly authenticated. A different system may use a "Y" in a different position to indicate an authenticated user. Each of those formats must be identified and registered on the database. While most vendors have standard default formats with the system, each time a new system or application is added those formats must be set up and activated.
- *Cross-referencing.* Not all users will be given access to all systems and applications. In some cases, it is possible to use groups of users to ease this effort. A user can be part of the "home office" group, and all applications can be linked together at the group level. In any case, groups must be identified and all access for each group must be set up for this to work.

The effort it takes to do user provisioning is sometimes either overlooked or underestimated in the drive to purchase and implement an SSO solution. Some vendors have in-house consulting staff dedicated to this effort; others may have identified firms that they recommend when it comes time to do the implementation. A rule of thumb to use in estimating this effort is that the provisioning work can be as high as three times the cost of the software.

Authentication and Single Sign-On

It is possible to confuse authentication systems and SSO applications and assume they mean the same thing. For example, some vendors will say theirs is an SSO system when it performs strong authentication and can be used to replace the default authentication system that comes with an operating system or server. This can be confusing for a businessperson or executive. A way to understand the difference and avoid confusion is to know that all SSO systems require authentication, but not all authentication systems can be used to provide SSO services.

Biometric authentication is a good application to use to illustrate this problem. A biometric system is a form of strong, two-factor authentication. It consists of something you know and something you are. In a typical implementation, a user is enrolled on a system and given a PIN number or password; he also registers his biometric identification, which can be a fingerprint, hand geometry, retina scan, or signature. When the user wants to access the system or resource, he enters his username and password (something he knows), and enters his biometric identification (something he is). This is considered a much stronger form of identification than a simple user ID and password system.

Given that this type of authentication is stronger (better) than user ID and password does not mean that it is the same thing as single sign-on. The authenticated user still has to be granted access to the target system or object. It is possible to use a biometric authentication system in a variety of ways. It can be used as the primary access control system in a normal one-to-one authentication scheme. It can also be used in conjunction with a directory-based SSO system in a one-to-many approach. The use of biometric authentication does not necessarily mean that there is an SSO system in use; it does mean that a stronger authentication system is in use.

The important point here is that authentication alone does not create an SSO system. Authentication is one service of such a system. Many companies that move to an SSO system for their business applications also require stronger authentication systems as a result of their concerns about the additional risk involved in single sign-on. This is seen as a way to get the best of both worlds — improved authentication while at the same time reducing overhead from multiple authentication systems.

This issue is one that the executive manager will likely have to confront. The business goals of productivity and efficiency can be met with the security goals of authentication and authorization through the proper implementation of an SSO system. It is up to the business executive and the security staff to ensure that both goals are met to guarantee the continued success of the business.

Chapter 11
Crisis Management: A Strategic Viewpoint

Introduction

The concepts around crisis management are neither new nor startling in their importance to the viability of any business. Yet the fact remains that many companies handle crisis management on an *ad hoc* basis and do not have formal plans in place to deal with anything beyond day-to-day problems. In the context of viewing the strategic issues in a business, it is important to define the role of crisis management and make the case for having a formal strategy in place to deal with serious incidents that affect business operations.

Business crises and problems come in all shapes and sizes, and most management teams are familiar with dealing with them as a normal course of business. At one end of the spectrum are the routine problems that come up on an almost daily basis — short-term outages, supply interruptions, staff comings and goings, etc. These are well within the normal scope of the duties of supervisory and middle management. At the other end of the spectrum are the major outages, the stuff that business continuity and disaster recovery plans are made for: fires, weather-related catastrophes, information technology infrastructure outages, and the like. Although not all companies have embraced formal plans to deal with these major interruptions, management and staff are well aware of them and have at least a rudimentary plan in mind to deal with them. These are so important that whole books have been written on how to plan for and survive them.

What is left on the table is a growing number of problems that come with a reliance on computers and computer systems for the basic business functions. The increase in computer-related incidents and computer system outages has lead to the development of a formal process to deal with them and this has become a more and more visible issue for executive management. This chapter discusses computer system incidents and puts them into a management perspective: the alternatives for successfully dealing with them.

The best resource in the United States for background information on this topic comes from Carnegie Mellon University and its CERT™ (Computer Emergency Response Team) organization (www.cert.org).*

It is important to note that although the basic framework for this discussion is dealing with computer-related incidents, the protocols and management discussion involved in this effort can apply to other types of crises and outages. The same basic concepts for reacting to a computer security incident can apply to a physical security incident or to any other breach in corporate rules or governance that is deemed severe enough to warrant a formal response process.

There are many organizational issues to be considered alongside this process. Is the organization under review a formal or an informal one? Is it a large, multi-layered organization, or is it a small, single-focused entity? Does the work of the business rely on computer systems and their related infrastructure, or are there other processes that are more important to the business in conducting day-to-day operations? These are good questions for the executive management team to keep in mind when discussing the need to develop a Computer Security Incident Response Team (CSIRT).

Crisis Management Questions for Corporate Executive Managers

1. How dependent is your business on its IT infrastructure?
2. How quickly do you need to have your company respond to an outage or computer security incident?
3. What is your policy toward releasing information about an incident to the public?
4. Who in your company has responsibility for crisis management?
5. Do you have formal plans in place to deal with a crisis?
6. Can you estimate the cost impact of an outage on your business?

Crisis Defined

This process starts with management defining the types of crises and situations that are considered important enough to warrant a formal response. Management should identify which issues require a formal response and which ones can be handled through routine procedures and policies. One of the definitions of a computer incident for this purpose is:

---

*CERT is a registered trademark of Carnegie Mellon University, and for the purposes of this discussion, one of the public domain terms for this idea, CSIRT (Computer Security Incident Response Team), will be used.

Any real or suspected adverse event in relation to the security of computer systems or computer networks; or, the act of violating an explicit or implied security policy. *

This is a good core definition to build on as part of this discussion. It covers a wide territory and points to the management issues that must be addressed.

Following is a list of the type of incidents covered here:

- Hacker attacks
- Privacy-related incidents
- Fraud
- Viruses, worms, and other computer malware
- Employee violations of security policy
- E-mail policy issues

Although each of these items can be explored in greater detail, the overall picture remains the same. It is the effect that such incidents has on the business that drives the decision of whether or not to develop a formal response mechanism. If the management of the business expects that it will have many incidents or that an incident will have a significant effect on the business, then a formalized response plan will make sense.

Measuring the impact of computer incidents on business is an inexact science at best. There have been many attempts at this through the years, but there is no standard established that crosses industry lines. Instead the generally accepted approach is to identify the cost drivers of a particular business and use them to craft a business impact assessment for the firm. Typical business impact assessment items include some or all of the following:

- Costs associated with an outage (lost business, impact on other projects or operations from the disruption, cost of using alternative processes, overtime of personnel involved with dealing with the outage)
- Remediation of systems or services as a result of the outage, including downtime from having to replace software or hardware damaged as a result of the outage
- System replacement costs
- Public relations issues, including press releases, customer notifications, and media response plans

There may be other items in this list that may be unique to a business. In the process of evaluating a need to develop a formal crisis management plan, one of the first steps in the planning process is to identify all the

*Computer Security Incident Response Team (CSIRT) Frequently Asked Questions, available at www.cert.org.

potential impacts on the business. The list that results from that analysis can become part of the formal cost justification for developing a CSIRT.

Also part of the discussion during this phase of the review is all the potential risk mitigation strategies that are included in the scope of crisis management. There are a number of strategies that overlap other areas of IT management that come into play at this point. For example, the many issues regarding e-mail processing and management should be part of this discussion, including firewalls, intrusion-detection systems, e-mail policies (including e-mail filtering), and file transfer policies (what will be permitted, what file types are forbidden, file size issues, and network capacity impact). All of these are part of the preventive and detective strategies associated with risk mitigation. Management should have as comprehensive a list of alternatives as possible to be able to choose the right alternative for its particular situation.

Other risk mitigation strategies include access control policies, physical security and perimeter security policies, and remote access policies and methodologies. The gathering together of each alternative may mean crossing organizational boundaries. Staff in the network area may feel they own the remote access strategy, and the physical security area may be the owner of access control systems. The organization issues will need to be set aside at this point as the overriding concern is corporate-level risk management and incident handling. Departmental and divisional procedures and plans will come later.

Beyond the policy issues are the crisis response strategies that are related parts of risk mitigation, including offsets through insurance, incident handling, legal liabilities, and disaster recovery planning. All of these activities can serve to lower the cost of an incident on the business once it occurs. Further information of risk mitigation and risk reduction alternatives can be found in Chapter 7, where that topic is discussed in detail. The information on disaster recovery can be found in Chapter 12; understanding that material is helpful in formulating a formal crisis response plan.

Benefits from a Formal Crisis Management Process

In many firms the crisis management process exists, although only in an informal manner. In those companies, the management team can often recite its plans for handling a crisis from memory even if it cannot point to any written plans or materials. The informal approach may be appropriate for that business, but that remains a decision for an informed executive management team. Moving from an informal to a formal process is not without cost. There are many organizational issues to consider, and as always, there should be benefits in mind of making changes to the organization. Those benefits are important, as they will serve as the justification for the formalizing of the plan and the level of effort needed to go from an informal plan to a formal one.

The benefits of formalizing the crisis management process are similar to those found in any quality improvement effort. The major benefit that management seeks is to minimize risk. This is done through reducing the response time once an incident occurs and also through having a formal process that will reduce the impact that any incident will have on the business. Charging an individual or a team with these responsibilities will provide the authority and support to document the organization's response to a problem, identify the types of problems that are occurring, and look for common threads in these incidents. The documentation becomes crucial going forward in the quantifying of events and finding the weaknesses in the organization that make it more vulnerable to other problems. Over time, the number of incidents should decrease, as should the impact of those incidents on the organization. Having the information in a single place allows management to track the process and measure progress.

Part of this process may already be in place in the organization. Most companies have some process in place to handle incidents and to notify management when they occur. The team assigned with creating a planned response process should look at past incidents and see what has been done; that material is a good place to start when examining the need for a formal crisis management response process.

Escalation and Notification

One of the most common ways to handle crisis management is with a simple escalation policy and notification plan. Many companies as they are growing have small, tightly knit groups of managers who work well together with a minimum of formality. When something bad happens, they can drop everything and rally around the area with the problem. They go through the standard problem-resolution process of "assess, assign, mitigate, and close." Relying on their in-depth knowledge of the business and their experience, they can be very successful at handling problems and reacting to a crisis.

An informal process works well until the organization outgrows it or the problems become repetitive and begin to impact productivity in other ways. Executive management should watch for signs that the problems in a business are outgrowing the current response process. These warning signs include repetitive problems or open issues that lack closure. Watching for the signs requires that the organization documents the problem management process or has a way for management to track problems at a high level by size, length of the outage, and a statement of the resolution of the problem.

Following is a list of crisis management reaction steps:

1. *Assess the problem.* This is always the first step; look at what has happened and make an initial judgment and reaction.
2. *Notify.* The next step is to decide whether the problem can be handled by the first responder; even so, there is a decision about notifying other affected parties.
3. *Assign.* The problem needs to be given to someone or to a group with the responsibility and capability to deal with the problem.
4. *Mitigation.* This is the obvious step of addressing the problem in the short run and trying to minimize the impact.
5. *Close out.* Once the problem has been addressed the documentation needs to be completed, showing what happened and how it was resolved.

There are other problems with this informal strategy that begin to emerge over time. The first issue comes with the assessment phase. Which problems get escalated? Who makes the decision about when to call for help? Without some advance planning, the initial reaction is to escalate everything so that management has tight control over events. This can quickly paralyze the company because soon everyone in the management team is involved in fire fighting and there is no one left to manage the day-to-day operations. The other problem is that the first responder may fall into the trap of waiting for management and not trying to solve things on his own. Time is of the essence during a crisis, and management should want the first responder to feel empowered and have the authority to take the right step immediately. Escalation is not the same thing as notification. The latter is a process whereby people inform others of actions that have occurred or need to occur. Escalation is the elevation of information to the next higher level of an organization with the assumption of action at the higher level. Notification can range from an after-action statement of the problem and the steps taken to resolve it, to alerting of other areas that may or may not be affected by the problem. Notifying those other areas allows them to invoke their response plans, which may in turn include escalation within their own management structure.

When considering if a CSIRT is needed in an organization, the executive team needs to look at the issues of escalation and notification as they already exist in the company. If there is already a notification and escalation plan in place, then that is something the CSIRT can build on as it moves forward. If those plans have been working to the satisfaction of the management team, the next issue is identifying the benefits that will come from further formalizing this process. What does management hope to gain by creating a new entity to deal with incident response? Ultimately, the answers to those questions are the keys to moving forward in this process and dealing with the organizational issues of crisis management.

Organizational Issues and Structures for Dealing with Crisis Management

Dr. Ron Barden, a professor at Georgia State University in Atlanta, theorized that there are five ways that people respond to a crisis:*

1. *Positive and helpful.* This is the ideal response and reaction. A person does something that helps resolve the situation and, through training or skill, does the right thing.
2. *Negative and helpful.* This is the next best approach to a crisis. A person does the right thing but does so with a less-than-positive attitude. A humorous way to describe this is a person who puts out the fire while complaining about spilling water on the floor.
3. *Positive and unhelpful.* This is a somewhat dangerous attitude. This describes a person who seems to be in control but does the wrong thing in a crisis. In this case, an example is someone who leaves the office during a crisis without telling anyone else there is a problem.
4. *Negative and unhelpful.* The worst-case human reaction: a person who does the wrong thing with the wrong frame of mind.
5. *Bizarre.* This behavior describes an unusual and unpredictable behavior pattern. The actions of this person during a crisis are completely unpredictable and therefore unreliable.

Looking at these possible responses is helpful in describing a framework and providing reasons why *ad hoc* reaction plans are highly risky. If there are no written plans, policies, or procedures, then the organization is totally dependent on the reaction of the first responder to the crisis. If the first person on the scene has the right training and the right reaction, then good things will happen. On the other hand, if the person lacks the skills, training, or attitude needed for a positive outcome, then the results become completely unpredictable. That is not a good thing to face when systems are down or customers are waiting for a service or product.

For the executive management team trying to formalize its approach to crisis management, there are several organizational models to review. Once the first step has been made to move from an informal to a formal structure, the next step is to look at any existing organizational roles to see if they can be applied to this effort and can become the model for crisis management. Other models, such as the CSIRT model, can then be studied and the right choice made to fit the business and its requirements.

As noted earlier in this discussion, the logical existing organizational model to look at is in the business continuity planning model and disaster recovery plan. Most companies with a mature IT infrastructure that are facing IT problems sufficient to warrant a crisis management approach

---

*Based on interviews and discussions with Dr. Barden in 1995 at SunTrust Banks, Inc., Atlanta, Georgia.

already have built a disaster recovery plan. In that plan are some of the same features as the crisis management plan: assess, notify, assign, mitigate, and close. Within the realm of business continuity planning, the disaster recovery plan documents similar steps, with notification plans and lists and escalation policies already in place. The difference is that the disaster recovery plan typically deals only with major, systemwide outages and is not well suited for small, short-duration, or local failures. The disaster recovery plan is also not designed to deal with many of the legal or public-relations issues associated with outages that a crisis management plan deals with.

Since the disaster recovery plan is at best only a starting place, the other choice is to look at the industry definitions of crisis management, such as a CSIRT. A CSIRT is a team within an organization that has the responsibility to provide a set of services in the event of a computer security incident such as a virus attack, hacking, and other specified violations of the corporate information security policy. The CSIRT, like the disaster recovery management team, is a limited-function task force within a company, in which membership is flexible based on the type of event and its impact on the business operations of the company.

Incidents that are typically assigned to a CSIRT for handling include major outbreaks of computer viruses, for example. In some companies, that may be as simple as sending out an e-mail reminder to verify that anti-virus software is up to date and whom to notify if a machine becomes infected. In other companies, the CSIRT may also be the group charged with quarantining the infected system, removing infected files, and repairing compromised systems. The CSIRT may also act as a clearinghouse for virus handling and may only be notified that an infection has occurred so that it can track infections and look for patterns of behavior that may indicate that policies need to be changed or training needs to be reinforced.

Another rule for a CSIRT is how to preserve a chain of custody for evidence from compromised systems and files. This is a more complex role than many people understand and may require the involvement of law enforcement and legal counsel. It is helpful in a situation like this that one member of the CSIRT is someone from the legal staff and another member is from the physical security staff; these departments typically have established relationships with local and state law enforcement agencies. Many people are familiar with these types of incidents through entertainment media. In real life, they do not occur as often as virus infections or even cases of internal misuses of computers. It is important to emphasize that the most critical management issue in this case is to understand the rules of evidence and evidence preservation. Someone in a company familiar with those rules needs to be part of the team to ensure the integrity of the evidence. Failure to preserve the chain of evidence makes future prosecution a moot point.

In either case, the critical role to define is that of the first responder to a security event. The first person notified or who discovers the problem is critical to its successful resolution. That person has a number of responsibilities, all of which should be documented as part of the crisis management plan, including:

- Notification
- Incident reporting and documentation
- Following the escalation guidelines
- Preservation of evidence
- Initial triage of the problem

These roles are not ones that can be taken lightly. The first few minutes after any incident is discovered can be critical to the successful resolution of the problem; so the training of the first responder and his understanding of his role are important. Each of the individual duties is critical to the successful resolution of the problem and the eventual resumption of normal operating guidelines.

As mentioned earlier, there is an overlap in responsibilities between the groups assigned with loss prevention and physical security. These groups already should have documented procedures in place that can be leveraged by the people assigned to the CSIRT. Those procedures should also be interfaced with other policies within the Human Resources and Public Relations departments. One of the long-held guidelines of disaster recovery planning is that no one should speak for the corporation other than the designated representatives of the PR or marketing areas. When there is a problem, the last thing a company needs is a comment from someone on the scene who does not have the whole picture. The loss prevention staff and the physical security staff are also well versed in this type of problem risk mitigation, and their involvement with the CSIRT will help minimize any mistakes that might be made in the heat of the moment.

A final word should be said at this point about outsourced services and their interaction with the operations of a CSIRT. More and more companies have outsourced parts of their operation, sometimes to organizations that are in different time zones or under different legal jurisdictions. Whenever this happens it is important to look at the potential impacts on crisis management. If there is a CISRT in existence, then its procedures and operations have to reflect those other entities. The escalation plans in that case need to work both ways that the company performing the service needs to know whom to contact and when to let them know there is a problem. This issue is discussed in greater depth in Chapter 15.

Strategies for Managing through a Crisis

There are many strategies for dealing with a crisis and its impact on a business. Although each incident has unique attributes, there are some common threads that go through security incidents and those can be used as models for the team to follow. Beyond assessment, notification, escalation, and resolution, there are two major areas that need to be discussed ahead of time — public relations and the legal department.

The Public Relations department is often the last area of a company to hear that there has been a problem. Due to a lack of understanding of its role, PR may not be notified about a problem at the same time as everyone else. The PR department has the training and the experience to help decide whom to notify and when to do it during a crisis. This experience can help prevent panic and can also avoid some potential liability from failure to properly notify the affected parties. California, for example, has recently enacted new legislation related to privacy laws, which requires companies to notify customers who live in California if there has been a breach of security that may impact the privacy of a customer's information.

There is a related task here that has to do with vendor notification and vendor management. If a company is the first one to experience a problem with a vendor's product, there are some conventions to follow about making the problem public. It has become customary to notify the product vendor first if one is involved in the incident. That has a twofold effect: first, it gives the vendor time to research the problem and propose a fix, prior to the public hearing about it; second, it minimizes to some degree the impact of the problem as it may not be well known that this problem exists. Premature release of the information may cause more damage, for example, as others may choose to exploit a weakness and use it for their benefit. This in turn can lead to further negative publicity about the victim.

The other group that has specialized knowledge is the legal department. There are many considerations in a security incident that need to be addressed by competent counsel. For example, privacy rights and evidence gathering are issues that should be left to a professional if there are any questions. Likewise, it is crucial to maintain a chain of evidence that can be supported in court if the company chooses to prosecute or if it turns the case over to law enforcement. Disk files can be copied to preserve their integrity as evidence, but merely reading them to see if data has been changed can render the files useless as evidence. Knowing what to do and when to do it is a critical task if the company seeks help through the judicial system. In that case, if it can be shown that the evidence had not been protected and had changed at some point, then the entire case may be thrown out of court.

These two areas can make a good case for formalizing incident handling procedures and developing a specialized team to deal with these cases. Part of the executive decision process should include discussions with legal counsel and public relations. Their involvement in the creation of such a plan is essential as they will be providing advice and direction of core plan elements.

Creating a Formalized Response for Crisis Management

Once the executive management team has reviewed its options, a decision can be made to move forward and create a formal crisis response plan. The size and scope of the plan must be sufficient to meet the needs of the company and not be seen as overly bureaucratic. The actual nature and type of crises vary, and the plan needs to remain somewhat flexible to fit the actual circumstances.

There are some good guidelines available if the chosen option is to organize around the CSIRT concept. That methodology provides a sound framework with a body of experience to fall back on during the development of the plan. The Carnegie Mellon CERT organization has a lot of material available for a company setting up its CSIRT, including a list of best practices using the following steps:

1. Obtain management support and buy-in.
2. Determine the CSIRT strategic plan.
3. Gather relevant information.
4. Design the CSIRT vision.
5. Communicate the CSIRT vision and operational plan.
6. Begin the CSIRT implementation.
7. Announce the operational CSIRT.
8. Evaluate the CSIRT effectiveness.*

This is a fairly standard set of steps for setting up any job function. The emphasis in this model, though, is on organizational issues such as executive management support and the creation of a vision and mission for the CSIRT. In many organizations, that part of the effort will take the minimum amount of time; once the project is approved no further action needs to be taken regarding executive management support and the vision for the CSIRT will be part of the documents that were used to justify its creation.

The hardest part of setting up a CSIRT may come in two areas. The first is gaining organizational support below the executive management level. A well-functioning CSIRT will require an ongoing commitment of time and effort by members of the team. Typically, those people will be assigned to the team on an as-needed basis, and when there are no active incidents to

---

* Creating a Computer Security Incident Response Team: A Process for Getting Started, available at www.cert.org.

deal with, the team members will have other routine job functions to perform. Their participation in team activities is analogous to volunteer firefighters; they will be expected to move rapidly from their regular role to their role as a team member when duty calls. Keeping them involved and available requires a commitment of resources that often crosses departmental or divisional lines in a company, which is why having support from the executive office is so important. If everyone knows and understands that the development and management of a CSIRT is a critical company effort, then everyone will make the necessary resources available to the effort.

The second challenge is to identify and manage the scope of work for which the CSIRT will be responsible. This will involve turf battles with other teams and areas already established within the organization. At the simplest level, virus incidents, the CSIRT will be interacting with the parts of the organization responsible for system support, the help desk and possibly the network management team; these groups interact on a daily basis with virus incident handling and management. The first question they may ask is about the added value of a CSIRT. At a more complex but lower-frequency level, there are incidents regarding hackers, systems intrusion, or information theft. These, in the mind of some people, are the type of events that a CSIRT is designed to handle. The challenge in these cases, though, is keeping the CSIRT relevant and up to date on its responsibilities while waiting for an opportunity to be called into action.

That may be the real challenge facing the team leader once the executive has made the decision to formalize the crisis management response process. Keeping the team focused in the absence of any activity can itself be stressful. Many incidents will be handled routinely as a course of doing business; the occasional virus report and the incidental attempt for unauthorized access are hardly worth convening a crisis management team. That is why the first steps in setting up a CSIRT or its equivalent are so important. The right team members with the right focus and understanding of the organization can make all the difference in the success or failure of the project. There is no real benefit to the company if the crisis management team becomes involved in routine, day-to-day operations, which, almost by definition, are not crises but operational issues. Documenting and tracking them may be a good function for the crisis management team. The documentation and the details of the actions taken can become good training material for the CSIRT and can also be used to look at operational issues that may be contributing to the problems. The tracking system used should interface directly with the same one used for routine problem management. Some customized data elements or screens may need to be added, but wherever possible the standard tracking system should be utilized. That way training costs can be held to a minimum while capitalizing on the efficiencies that are possible due to staff familiarity with existing systems.

The final step listed in this plan is therefore an important one — evaluating the effectiveness of the CSIRT. This should be done on a regular basis using preapproved metrics for performance measurement. For example, incident response times should be tracked and measured, as should cost issues. Staff time and costs should be tracked on a per-incident basis as well as on a total-cost basis. In larger companies, there are often expense tracking and cost recovery systems to deal with. The expenses of the CSIRT may be allocated in those cases to a general overhead account, or they can be billed back to the product or profit line that was affected.

There also should be a periodic review on the whole concept. Is the time and effort justified in maintaining a CSIRT? Are there lessons learned that have contributed to an overall quality improvement process? Are there fewer incidents or more over time? How have the costs per incident been tracking; are they up or down? All of those are valid measurements for an effort of this significance. If a CSIRT is to be established, then it must fit within the normal corporate operating criteria.

Conclusion

It is important that the executive management team is fully involved in crisis management. The idea of forming a formal response process for computer incidents has to have more than the usual letter of support from the CEO; it has to have his or her understanding of the issues and the commitment to make it work. That commitment needs to be shared with the rest of the business to ensure their support and cooperation in this effort. Periodically, other issues may arise that will challenge that ongoing commitment, and management should be prepared ahead of time to understand those potential conflicts and to respond to them quickly.

The lack of understanding or commitment can lead to this missing the real benefits that can come from this process. A fully functioning formal response to a crisis can reduce the impact, lower the cost, and lead to fewer incidents in the future, goals that any executive team wants as part of its organization.

Chapter 12
Business Continuity Planning

Introduction

Business continuity planning (BCP) is the modern-day successor of what had been called disaster recovery management. This change occurred over the last decade as more and more companies expanded their view of what is necessary to keep their doors open in the face of both natural and man-made problems. This expanded view has meant that, as it is understood today, disaster recovery is a subset of business continuity planning.

The major difference between the two is that business continuity is all about planning ways to keep the doors open while minimizing the impact of disruptions on customers and business operations. Disaster recovery management is the series of steps taken to restore the business once a problem occurs. In recent times, the preparations for the year 2000 date change were a good example of BCP, and the events of September 11, 2001, touched on disaster recovery.

Specialists in this field, such as Sungard Recovery Services, have taken this idea a step further. According to Ken Simone, a recovery planning expert at Sungard, the new term in use is "business continuity continuum." In this view, the recovery process is looked at over the time it takes to recover critical records vs. the investment in the recovery process. At the low end are traditional tape recovery systems and at the high end are managed backup and recovery processes. The BCP planner working with the business unit managers then tries to match the recovery process with the criticality of the business function. In that sense, recovery ceases to be a one-size-fits-all process and is customized for each area. That is an important new approach as it allows executive management to have a more granular approach to risk reduction and places emphasis on risk management rather than disaster planning.

A related idea proposed by the experts is that the planning, testing, and execution of a business continuity plan are a constant and ongoing effort that has to reflect changes in the makeup of the business and changes in the threats that the business faces. Recovery plans have to be made more flexible so that they can change with the changes in business activities. This will put more pressure on the planning process as it means more work on the front end to understand the business and its goals and objectives. The old idea of a static planning process has to be abandoned in order to meet the challenges of today.

Executive management should expect that it has a significant role in the development and approval process of contingency plans as part of its job. It is no longer possible for a CEO to relegate these tasks to people in the IT department or in buildings and facilities. It is part of the CEO's job today to report to the Board on preparations for risk management and reaction to events that are beyond the normal course of business. This expanded role means that the CEO should be involved in these preparations and should have a full understanding of the impact of disasters and outages on his business.

There are also other strategies and policies that impact the plans and preparations done as part of the BCP. For example, one of the key steps is to identify all assets of the company and develop a risk profile for those assets. Another step requiring input from the executive suite is the high-level decisions regarding recovery strategies and contingency plans. Decisions to build or buy a backup site, or choosing which currently automated tasks can be done manually in a disaster and which need to remain automated are all key business decisions as opposed to operational or technical decisions. The implementation of those decisions remains at the operational level, but making the choices and allocating the funds needed to execute those plans is best done with the full knowledge and support of the executive team.

As mentioned at the outset, disaster recovery is a subset of business continuity planning. Most people are more familiar with disaster recovery and often assume that the two are synonymous. The simplest way to explain the difference is that a disaster recovery plan is aimed at getting specific business functions back up and running in the event of an outage. Typical disaster recovery plans are ones involving recovering data center operations at a new location in the event the regular location becomes unusable. A business continuity plan encompasses all aspects of the business, including data center recovery. It is aimed at providing a near-seamless set of services to the customer and making sure that the business continues to function in the event of a problem or outage.

At the outset of the process certain assumptions need to be made and put in writing as they will shape and drive the process. Those assumptions have to do with things like the scope of the plan, the timeline for recovery, and the ability of the company to withstand outages of various types.

Those assumptions may be challenged along the way and it is important that they be drafted at the start of the process so that all the components of the plan will be done on the same basis.

One of the key elements of this process starts with the building of a risk profile for a company. Each company will have a unique risk profile, even within an industry. The process to develop this profile starts with an understanding of what types of events will be considered in the planning process.

Types of Outages and Disasters Outages

When developing a business continuity plan, the first step is to put some parameters around what type of events the plan covers. The major types are natural disasters and man-made events. All areas to be covered will fall into one of these two categories, and each business will need to determine which of these events apply to it.

The following list of natural disasters is the one that most people are familiar with when talking about a continuity plan:

- Floods
- Earthquakes
- Fire
- Weather events such as tornados, hurricanes, ice, hail, and wind
- Landslides, avalanches, and other earth movements

This list is one that most people are familiar with as they also have to deal with it in their personal life. Homeowners are familiar with preparing their family for these kinds of events and are also familiar with the need to have protection against the occurrence of fires and floods. In business, the risks expand as there are events in other parts of the country that can impact a business more directly than it would impact an individual. Key suppliers in one part of the country, for example, may face a natural disaster that does not affect their customers in a different part of the country.

Business today uses the following list of man-made disasters, which has grown in recent years to include computer-related events:

- Sabotage of property, computer systems, and information
- Terrorist acts
- Strikes
- Protests and other forms of civil unrest
- Denial-of-service attacks on computer networks
- Viruses, worms, and other computer beasts

This list sounds more like a set of criminal acts and in many ways it is, because some of these events involve legal issues beyond the scope of routine business decisions. Protests can shut down streets or other transportation systems. Hackers can attack networks that affect suppliers and customers. The common thread in this list is that each of them can be traced back to actions by people. The risks to any one business from any one threat may vary greatly based on location, type of business, and product or suppliers.

There is a third group of disasters that are a subset of natural disasters and man-made events:

- Infrastructure failures (utility outages, power outages, etc.)
- Communications failures (including internal and external hardware as well as software and networks)
- Transportation outages (airport closures or limitations, road closures, etc.)

This third group is often included in the natural disaster list as these outages are thought of as more widespread or as affecting more than one business. Recent events point to these outages as needing special attention, however. For example, after September 11, 2001, many businesses had to deal with the suspension of air travel in the United States. Companies had to find ways to get business travelers home. Travel-related industries had to deal with the collapse of their own system. Hotels, resorts, and airport concessionaires had to revise their business plans in the face of the suspension of air travel over an indefinite timeframe. The latter point is what made that particular outage so difficult to deal with. In most natural disasters, there are some defined limits to the disaster — the storm is over, the flood has passed, and life returns to normal. The recovery plan can be executed against a background of normalcy except for the outage caused by the event. In the aftermath of September 11, 2001, no one knew when "normal" would return. How long should you defer travel? How long should you leave your business traveler out on the road before you take extraordinary methods to bring him home?

There are other recent events that have the same uncertain property. Hazardous materials spills caused an area to be evacuated. Bioterrorism shut down mail service in the United States. Critical documents were caught in limbo, waiting for delivery. Companies had no way of knowing when, if ever, those materials would be delivered. Some of the challenges they faced was to decide if they should resend materials using couriers or if they should negotiate for delays in contracts and agreements. The uncertainty of these events was a great challenge to everyone.

Whatever the type of outage, or the origin, the effect on any business can be debilitating. Failure to develop a plan and execute it in a crisis can make the difference between an ongoing concern and having to close the doors.

Planning for a Disaster

The responsibility for the ongoing operation of a business rests at the highest level of the organization. The definition of a corporation, after all, is "an entity with an infinite life." To fulfill the duties that go with that responsibility, the Board of Directors must hold management accountable to develop a reasonable plan to ensure the long-term viability of the organization.

Management, in turn, can delegate the development and maintenance of such a plan to the appropriate professionals within the organization. That may mean assigning the responsibility for business continuity planning to a lower level within the organization structure while maintaining approval authority at a higher level. What it should not mean is abdicating the responsibility for the plan. The CEO and executive team need to be part of the plan and need to understand their roles in the development and execution of such a plan. It is a common mistake in many businesses to delegate the planning and approval process. With the advent of increased Board of Directors' oversight through legislation such as the Sarbanes–Oxley Act, management must acknowledge that it retains the responsibility for the actions of subordinates. With respect to business continuity planning, this should mean that management understands the content of the plan, not just the fact that it exists.

The cost of developing a plan will vary greatly from business to business, and it is up to executive management and not some lower level in the company to ensure that the plan is correct. Funding to develop the plan is just the start of the process, and management must make the financial resources available to ensure the successful execution of the plan.

The steps in developing such a plan are simple and the same, regardless of the type of industry or the size of the business:

- Recovery strategy development (identifying the minimal acceptable recovery configuration)
- Business impact analysis
- Critical resources identification
- Information protection strategy
- Business continuity plan development
- Plan implementation
- Testing and maintenance

Each of these steps has numerous issues for management that will be discussed further. The critical issue at this point is to understand that the plan has to be a living document, not just something that sits on the shelf. As such, it will require that management allocates the appropriate resources for its development and maintenance. Those resources include a level of funding, the right team makeup, and the support of the management team. Support from the executive office cannot be underestimated. Without the full backing of the executive team, critical issues may be ignored or deferred that may ultimately impact the survival of the business.

A word of caution at this point is also appropriate. If a company is in danger of going out of business for other reasons, such as financial setbacks or resource limitations, it is clear that work on the business continuity plan may be deferred. That may be a correct decision, but it must be made at the highest level of the company. If the company is in danger of imminent collapse, then clearly the executive team should no longer be thinking it is dealing with an ongoing concern, and having an up-to-date contingency plan is a luxury that it cannot afford. On the other hand, there are some measures that could be put in place even at that point that will ensure that critical functions survive to keep the business going. Those steps may be as simple as having the information technology staff back up a disk drive, thus ensuring that copies of critical documents are available to be stored off site. Work on developing a more robust plan can be deferred for a time when there are resources available and the viability of the company is less of a concern.

The reason for mentioning the preceding situation is to move that discussion off the table. Too often the development of a business continuity plan will be deferred for a rainy day in light of other, seemingly more pressing problems. The business continuity plan is intended to ensure the business survives to see that future day and deferring the development of a plan is not a valid option. The duty of developing a plan, no matter how rudimentary, is no different than management's other fiduciary responsibilities.

The steps listed previously are generalized to suit this level of discussion. It is important to note that the planning process is similar to almost any other project management effort. The first step is the justification and the goal setting. The plan is then estimated and cost issues are decided. These steps show why it is important to have executive management support and oversight. There are many alternatives to be reviewed before the plan is written, and each of those alternatives needs to be evaluated and the proper one selected for the plan to be effective. Placing responsibility for the plan at too low a level in the organization will negatively impact the ability to make those decisions on a timely basis. This is critical as the next phase requires that resources are assigned to create the plan and they execute the project plan. The last steps include testing the plan and then having a process to revise and update the plan as necessary.

This chapter does not go into the details of developing a sound continuity plan. Instead, the intent is to discuss the issues regarding continuity planning. This means it is necessary to discuss all aspects about a plan and to describe the planning process. There are available a number of resources for use in the planning process that describes the details in greater depth. Those resources are important and should be used by the person responsible for the plan. There are now certifications available for planning professionals to measure their knowledge of this sometimes difficult subject. There are a number of consulting companies that can provide skilled personnel and planning templates that will make this process easier and move it along more quickly. Decisions on using consultants, inside talent, or skilled professionals are ones that need to be made by senior management as part of its commitment to the business recovery planning process.

Roles and Responsibilities

The first real step after deciding to develop a plan is to assign the roles and responsibilities for the plan. As in any major effort, there should be an executive sponsor of the plan who will take responsibility for the success of the plan from start to finish. In many companies that will be the Chief Financial Officer. The assignment of this plan to the CFO makes sense as the early phases of the plan deal with risk management and assumptions about the business impact analysis (BIA). Other choices are the Chief Technology Officer or the head of internal audit. There is a good case to be made for either position.

The CTO has responsibility for critical IT resources, and in many companies those are the ones that will get the most attention in a continuity plan. On the other hand, the CTO usually does not have responsibility for operational resources or for buildings and facilities. The CTO's overall scope is limited and he may not understand other key business issues that should be incorporated into a comprehensive plan. If asked to develop a plan, the CTO will usually place emphasis on the protection of technology-based assets at the expense of others, such as business records and operational facilities.

The head of internal audit faces similar hurdles if he becomes responsible for the BCP. Audit, like it or not, is usually seen in an adversarial light. Audit also generally lacks credibility with the operational and information technology staff to make decisions about operational issues or nonfinancial risk management issues. Audit can and should be a major contributor to the plan, however, and needs to be part of the development team.

The CFO position has the most visibility and the greatest chance to influence the plan from a corporatewide perspective. There are many issues that make the CFO the best qualified of the executive team to act as sponsor for the plan:

- Choosing alternatives such as when to use insurance as part of the risk mitigation strategy
- Judging the impact of an outage on the financial viability of the business, which is a key part of the BIA
- Assessing regulatory issues and their affect on risk management
- Assessing cost issues and recommending budget and cost guidelines

The role of the executive sponsor should not affect the assignment of the responsibility for the work involved in developing the plan, however. Organizational choices at that level will vary greatly from industry to industry. In some cases, the best place will be in an operational area, particularly if there are buildings or property issues that need to be considered. Likewise in a technology-centric company, the Chief Information Officer's organization may be the best place for the planning function. Those issues are also good ones to be discussed and settled at the CFO level.

Once the executive sponsor has been identified and the organizational issues settled, there are some other structural issues to work through. Depending on the size of the organization, the continuity plan may be simple or complex. In large organizations with multiple business lines and facilities, the BCP may need to have a separate committee that oversees the planning process and acts as both manager of the plan and manager of the planning process. In smaller organizations, those functions may reside in the office of the person responsible for writing and updating the plan itself. In either case, management of the planning process needs to be thought through and designed with the business in mind.

For example, in a large company that has many operating divisions across many locations there will usually be a management team that controls the entire planning process. The team will make decisions on recovery priorities and even make the first decision on cost–benefit issues in the planning process. That team exists on an everyday basis and will also review test strategies and results when the time comes.

The plan itself will bring up the creation of numerous other teams that form the core components of the plan and recovery process. Some of the teams that will be created include:

- Recovery management team (sometimes called the incident management team). This team will be activated at the time of a disaster. Its job is to execute the disaster recovery plan and get the critical functions of the business restored as soon as possible.
- Salvage team. This team goes on site in the event of a disaster to decide what can be salvaged and what needs to be replaced. This can include assessing paper records and computer files as well as the facilities that house them.

- Operational team. These are the people who run things until the business returns to normal. Usually this team is a subset of the team that has the day-to-day responsibilities for running the same functions under normal circumstances.
- Communications team. This team designs the means of communicating information to employees, customers, and the public in general. This team takes into account what types of things can be said and by whom. This is critical in the first days of an outage as there will be a greater demand for information, and it occurs at a time when the normal channels are disrupted by the outage itself.

All of these roles need to be reviewed and primary and backup personnel should be identified; lists of these teams and their contacts then become core documents in the plan. Once the teams have been identified and have met, the planning process begins in earnest and other management issues will surface.

Plan Alternatives and Decision Criteria

Once the organizational issues have been decided, the planning process moves to an evaluation phase, in which the critical resources of the company are identified and their risk profiles are developed. This is an important point where the executive sponsor's involvement will once again be needed.

Creating or using an already existing inventory of corporate assets is a simple process. This can be time-consuming, however, depending on the availability of information. Key to this step is the identification of the systems that are deemed critical to running day-to-day operations. This inventory is usually built around lists of hardware, software, and networks that come from the IT organization, and should only be thought of as a starting point as there are many other areas that may have critical infrastructure items.

Part of the background material needed in this step is the creation of a criticality rating system that will be used to set recovery priorities. A typical scheme is to rate all items on a 1 to 10 scale with the most critical items receiving a "1" rating and the least critical receiving a "10." Likewise, a rating system needs to be assigned to rate the risk for each of those systems. Some systems rated "1" for criticality may have a low risk rating. The risk of occurrence is not important in the discussion at this point as that deals with the issue of frequency of a problem. The risk here deals with the total risk affecting a system or business process. Using a dual rating system allows the segregation of these ideas, which is important to help assure the fairness of the rating process. This will eventually be used to create a recovery priority scheme as part of the disaster recovery plan. Not all systems or operations can be recovered on day 1 after a disaster, and it is important to have a list in priority order for recovery to ensure that the critical functions are recovered first.

This can be a very politically charged process. All managers like to believe that their systems and functions are business critical. They also are afraid that a low rating of criticality will affect senior management's perception of their importance to the organization. Some recovery planners have had people react to the process as if it were a threat to their job or that it might lead to layoffs if the criticality of their job were too low. This process should be explained from the outset as one that is independent, having nothing to do with the rating of a manager or the rating of the area's or function's importance to management. This process is about business continuity and business resumption planning. A good example is the volatility of this discussion that can occur over the rating of the Human Resources area and its functions. With respect to disaster recovery planning, the HR area usually ranks low in importance, because in the short run there may be little activity in HR operations. Most executives, though, would agree that payroll is important from a business continuity standpoint, and employees will not work long without being paid for their services. A complication to this ranking is that many companies have outsourced their payroll systems and they retain only an interface to the service provider and no longer have much if any of the payroll information residing on their internal systems. In this case, HR might rank as a low priority, a 4 to 5, with a lower risk rating because the processing is done through a service provider. But to stay in business the management team recognizes that payroll must be available soon after an outage or employees will stay home and the business will fail. As in every process that the planner will examine, there are some work-around solutions that might apply in a disaster that would otherwise be considered bad management practices. For example, payroll checks can be issued based on the most recent timesheet an employee submitted and then adjusted once the crisis period has passed and operations are back to normal.

This process continues throughout the organization and it applies to business functions as well as to their supporting systems and infrastructure. This is combined with the risk assessment process. In this process, two issues are considered and combined to create the risk profile of the business. The first part is to look at the potential threats to the business. The list of natural and man-made disasters at the outset of this chapter is the framework for this process. Each business function is considered for the likelihood of that risk occurring. In many cases, these are all combined together as most systems or operating functions occur in the same location, and the likelihood of any risk occurring will be similar for all functions in that one location. It may also be important at this point to prioritize which areas will get their recovery plans completed first. This same information can be used to create a schedule for developing the recovery plans based on the ordination of their risk profile information.

The risk profile is then used together with the criticality rating to help with providing a cost-effective risk mitigation process. In the context of business continuity planning, all the most important systems with a high-risk profile should get the most attention. Strategies are then considered to minimize the risk and to help ensure that those functions remain in operation to protect the company. The less critical functions then get reviewed and a strategy is created for every part of the business. This also applies to the selection of the recovery methodology. In some cases, there is a need to have significantly faster recovery times than in others. Those decisions should be risk based and incorporated into the planning process.

This may seem very complicated and time-consuming, but it should also be remembered that once this is done it only needs to be maintained and reviewed on a regular basis. It does not need to be recreated from the ground up. If there are major changes in the business or the business operations, then the plan will need to be revised to reflect the new situation. Part of the idea of a business recovery continuum is to imbed the business continuity planning process into all forms of project management. If the business merges or divests itself of a business process or subsidiary, then the business continuity plan must be updated for all affected parties. Likewise if there is any change in operations, such as new forms or equipment, this would also require a review and update of the continuity plan. Changes in technology also mean changes in business process. The sooner a company realizes that business continuity is a core function and strategic to the survival of business, the better the plan will be and the more useful it will be in a crisis situation.

Risk Mitigation vs. Risk Elimination

It is rarely practical to eliminate risk completely in business. In most cases, it is only practical to select a cost-effective approach to risk mitigation and apply that to the business continuity plan. This does not mean that creating a paper plan that has no hope of success is a valid strategy; it does mean that management should look at all alternatives and make an informed decision based on risk tolerance.

For example, a company could build completely redundant operations in multiple locations and have them run 24/7 with a hot switch over capability. The cost would likely be prohibitive, however, and would put such a great financial strain on the business that it would not survive. A more practical approach is to have a mix of recovery strategies in place that is matched against both the criticality and risk profiles of each business function and operation.

Following is a list of some of the risk mitigation strategies that are available:

- Fire suppression and fire prevention equipment
- Perimeter security and other physical security mechanisms
- Insurance
- Hot sites, cold sites, and warm sites for computer systems
- Spare equipment
- Off-site storage of critical information
- E-vaulting (an updated approach to off-site file storage that makes use of prevalent high-speed networks to have real-time backup and recovery of critical files, useful in cases where a high degree of system availability is important)
- Inventory management systems and alternate supply sources
- Records retention policies and off-site storage of critical records

This list is not comprehensive but is intended to be used as part of the planning process and to emphasize the importance of this as a management function. All those strategies have a cost associated with them. Once the risk profiles have been created, the risk mitigation strategies are reviewed and the appropriate ones are selected for each area. This may involve some negotiation as the cost of risk mitigation has to be balanced against the risk profile. In some cases, this may mean accepting more risk than in another area. It may be appropriate to use insurance alone as the risk mitigation strategy for one area while another may need a fully redundant site to operate in the event a disaster occurs.

Changes in recovery technologies will also affect the risk mitigation strategy that the firm chooses. The most recent change is the advent of E-vaulting and managed online backup services. This type of service makes use of cheap network bandwidth that has become available to allow both faster movement of information off site and faster recovery of the data when needed. The benefits from this process can include reducing the recovery time from hours to minutes and moving the burden for administration of the file backup process to a trusted third party who specializes in that business. It remains the responsibility of the client, however, to manage that relationship and continue to test the continuity plan. Having a third party handle the backup process does not guarantee that the plan will work when it is needed.

The fiduciary role of the executive comes into play at this point. The senior management team and the Board of Directors may have to be consulted when completing this part of the process. The management team assigned to create the plan may be unwilling to accept the risks and may want to have additional mitigation measures in place that the senior management team may feel can wait for a more profitable time in the life of the business. This is why it is a strategic issue, not a tactical one, and why it is important that the executive team is fully involved in this process.

Preparation: Writing the Plan

The writing of the plan and the documents that will make it up is a more or less mechanical process at this point. There are a number of excellent sources of information to guide this process, including samples of the various forms and details of the processes that make up a good plan. A good source of this information is *Business Continuity Planning* by Ken Doughty (Auerbach Publications, 2000), which contains a wealth of information that can be used in the guidance and development of a sound continuity plan.

The people writing the plan can come from either the operations area, from an external source such as a consultant, or from the staff within the area for which the plan is being written. Some contingency planning professionals believe that the plan must be written by the actual staff in the area to create a proper sense of ownership as well as to help ensure the accuracy of the plan. This may or may not be true, but in the long run what is important is that the plan is created and put into action. The accuracy of the plan can be addressed through testing and auditing. The sense of ownership can come from the sense of accountability that executive management creates in the minds of the managers.

What is important in the context of this book is to remember that the plan is a living document and that it needs to be part of the business plan. Each document in the plan should be dated and signed by the creator and the approving body. That way an audit of the plan can be done later to ensure that it is current and that it reflects the actual operations of the business. All businesses are in a constant state of change, and only if the plan is dated can it be identified with respect to the state of the business.

Testing and Auditing the Plan

Testing the plan and measuring its effectiveness is as important or perhaps more important as creating the plan. A plan that has never been tested may have significant failure points and may expose the business to undue risk. An untested plan can also create a false sense of security. This is the same principle as learning the need to test the smoke detector in the home or office. The detector sits on the wall and appears to be working, but a test may reveal that the batteries have failed and the detector is not functioning.

There are a variety of ways to test a plan. These tests do not have to be costly or interrupt the daily operation of the business. The result of the test should also be looked at not as one of pass/fail but more in terms of the evolution of the plan. Finding out about weakness in a plan as the result of testing is certainly better than as a result of a real disaster.

Some testing alternatives include:

- *Paper test.* This may be as simple as discussing the plan at a staff meeting in light of current events. The important thing is to document the discussion and to use any lessons learned as part of the process to improve the plan.
- *Structured walk-through.* This is where a team goes through the plans using different scenarios under the supervision of the planning team.
- *Component test.* In this test, each part of the overall plan may be tested independently. The results are then looked at to see how the overall plan might have worked if all components were tested simultaneously.
- *Simulation.* In this type of test, the teams are given a scenario to follow that presents real-world cases to them. In general, this does not include actually moving to an alternate location but may include simulating utility outages as a way to see how complete a plan may be.
- *Disaster recovery exercise.* This is the type of test that most people in IT are familiar with and may have participated in at some point in their career. In this test, the plan is activated and computer systems are switched to their backup systems, which may include running at alternative sites. This is sometimes called a "parallel" test as the production systems will remain functional while the recovery systems are brought up and their functionality is tested.

In all cases, it is important to start off with a simple plan for testing and then increase the scope of the test gradually. Each time, though, the following items are important to remember:

1. Identify the scope and goals for the test.
2. Document the test plan and the results.
3. Review the results with the participants and write up the lessons learned from the test.
4. Update the plan based on the results of the test.

This process is the same whether you are talking about the back-office operations of the Finance department or you are talking about the operations of the network management group. The important thing to remember is that the plan will only be effective if it is accurate and up to date and reflects the actual conditions of the business. Likewise, the tests are only useful if they too reflect actual conditions and if the results of the test are used to improve the plan.

The goal of testing is not to succeed or fail. The goal of testing is to improve the plan and also to help train the people who will execute the plan. A test that was 100 percent successful is one that probably was not ambitious enough or does not accurately reflect real-world conditions. Likewise, a test that "failed" may actually be better for the organization as it is one that showed the weaknesses in the plan prior to having to use the plan in the event of a real interruption or disaster.

The Audit department also has an important role in this effort. Auditing the plan and the planning process, though, is not a substitute for testing the plan. Auditing the process is important as it helps ensure that the plan is complete and that all areas of the company have been examined and brought into the process. Audit can also look at the assumptions of the plan and challenge those as necessary. Audit is important for independent oversight for the testing process. Auditors should be present during tests as often as practical. They can serve as referees when test scripts and assumptions come under fire during the execution phase of the test. Likewise, the auditor can look across the entire organization and see that plans are consistent and the planning process has been done with similar levels of quality. This is especially critical in larger organizations where different areas may not have done a good job of communicating during the planning process.

It cannot be repeated too often that the success or failure of this process depends on more than the just the support of management; it depends on its involvement in the entire process. From setting goals to setting priorities, it is executive management who can and should be a key part of the process.

Issues for Executive Management

Beyond involvement in the planning process, executive management will likely face a number of issues as a result of the business continuity planning process. These are issues that should be discussed at the highest levels of the company, and the results of those communications can be passed along to the relevant managers.

There are a number of operational issues that will come up in this process. Inventory levels, alternate suppliers, and staffing levels will be discussed as part of the business continuity plan. For example, the level of inventories may need to be adjusted in light of recent world events if a company wants to stay at the same level of production after a disaster occurs. That is not a simple decision as it may impact issues from transportation to storage to cost of doing business. Those are nontrivial decisions and will affect the bottom line of the company.

Other operational issues may include looking at the effect of expanding the business, the choice of location for critical facilities, or the change out of equipment. It is not unusual for a business to find that the new equipment it has bought is more modern than anything it has in inventory to use in a disaster recovery scenario. That may mean that the company has to choose between a degraded operation in the event of a disaster and having to buy and warehouse expensive equipment to ensure a timely, full recovery of a critical function.

Delegation of authority is another issue for executive management to deal with in the planning process. During a disaster the reality is that it may be completely impractical to go through the normal chain of command to buy something. The usual spending limits and duplicate signature process may be impossible to follow if phone lines are down or alternative suppliers have to be utilized. Management needs to be made aware of these issues and the appropriate decisions made and control processes in place to deal with these events. It may be prudent to allow the on-site personnel to spend any amount needed to keep the business running, but there also needs to be accountability for those expenses and a way to reconcile them once things return to normal.

Returning to normal is an area of importance that is often overlooked. Once the disaster or outage has passed and the company is functioning, there needs to be a plan in place to return to normal operation. That may involve days or weeks of effort to ensure that records are maintained in two locations and that the switchover is done in a way that customers are not impacted a second time. There is one well-known case of a banking institution that tried to switch back from disaster mode to regular process and found that it did not have a good audit trail of customers' transactions. Once the bank returned to regular processing, customers complained that their accounts were no longer up to date and did not reflect recent activity. This was embarrassing, and it also allowed some unscrupulous customers to defraud the bank of hundreds of thousands of dollars that the bank had no way to track. A way to avoid a problem like that is to use the recovery plan as a guideline to build the more comprehensive plan to return to normal operations. The same priorities that were used to write the plan should apply to returning to normal once the plan has been invoked.

The final major issue for executive management is to integrate business continuity planning with business planning. This means that strategic-level decision making should take into account the issues of keeping the company running on a day-to-day basis. Spinning off a division or closing a plant are major decisions that the executive management team will spend a lot of time considering. The executive team will look at the financial case and the impact on customers and on the owners of the business; it also needs to consider the effect of such decisions on the business continuity plan. Pieces of a company often supply critical services to each other and may serve key elements in each other's disaster recovery plans. Spinning off a business may make sense and may be the prudent thing to do, but all the impacts of that decision need to be examined and any effects that it has on the business continuity plan should be documented.

This may mean that some other affected area will incur higher costs once the divestiture has occurred. That area may now have to get in contact with an external service provider to replace the services performed by the former peer division of business line in the event of a disaster. Those costs need to be associated with the decision that caused them to occur. Otherwise, the affected area may defer the expense, leaving an exposure and new risks to the business where none existed before.

The same issues apply with respect to acquisitions and business expansion. In buying another company, the management team may find that this can be an opportunity to lower risk through the use of alternate sites or through the use of excess resources that come with the new acquisition. In this case, the plans of the company will also have to be revised with the potential for saving money in mind.

Conclusion

Business continuity planning is one of the areas executive management needs to view as an opportunity to delegate decision making while retaining authority for major issues. One of the critical considerations for executive management is the cost of the plan. Companies can cut spending on the recovery process, creating risks that the plan was designed to eliminate.

Business continuity planning is a process that at the outset may appear to be a simple one but upon further examination can be seen as complex. It is a process that has a lot of exposure and a real need for executive support and involvement. Failure to do so may increase the risk the company faces instead of reducing it, as was the intent with the creation of the plan.

Chapter 13
Security Monitoring: Advanced Security Management

Introduction

In the evolution of an effective information security program, the first steps have to do with evaluating risks and setting policies. After that, there are numerous areas that the security professional moves into such as the implementation of an authentication scheme, e-mail protection (virus scanning, content filtering, etc.), and network protection strategies (firewalls, intrusion-detection systems, etc.). Another important part of this process involves testing the effectiveness of those steps and analyzing the results of those tests. Each of these steps produces a tremendous amount of information providing feedback that the security management team must analyze and react to over time.

Typically, those reactive steps come in the form of a CSIRT (Computer Security Incident Response Team, discussed in Chapter 11), where management has a team of trained professionals who analyze the information and formulate a response plan. This requires that the CSIRT is available at a moment's notice and that it has the training and knowledge needed to recognize the difference between a real security alert and a false alarm. Yet another challenge to management that also forces a reactive strategy comes from the results of audits. When a company has gone through an audit, the report provides a snapshot of the weaknesses and vulnerabilities that exist. Again, management must have the properly trained staff available to understand what the auditor is talking about and formulate an appropriate response. In both of these cases, all this work is done after a problem has been found. The problem can take the form of a security breach, a security alarm, or a negative comment by the auditor. Each of these problems takes time and effort for someone to research.

There is a potentially better way to look at the volumes of data that are coming in, and that is to find a proactive way to deal with it through security monitoring.

Security monitoring here is defined as the ability to review and evaluate computer security information and events in a timely manner to formulate an effective response. Looking at audit reports and reviewing security alerts is not monitoring. Waiting for the alarm is a reactive step. Monitoring in this context is more proactive; it means looking at the available forms of information that security professionals receive and then feeding that input to a larger information system. That information system then is both a repository and a decision tool for the security professional. When properly designed and managed, this system will improve the productivity of the security manager while reducing the level of effort it takes to identify weaknesses before they become problems.

This is a concept that is currently gaining more and more proponents. Many vendors today use the terms "security monitoring," "security console" or "dashboard" to describe their products. The term that is emerging to describe these products as a group is "security information management" or SIM. SIM products from different vendors share some similar concepts such as the use of software agents running on the different products and systems that are to be monitored. The agents then send messages to a server that is running the security management console. The agent software can use intelligent agents that perform some local filtering of the monitored events prior to collection, or the agent can merely act as a traffic monitor that passes all information back to the monitoring server in a common format. In either case, there is a software-based security console that analyzes the information, producing reports, charts, and even real-time alarms as necessary.

The security console is monitored by a person who reviews the consolidated alerts and alarms, judges the severity of the incident, and takes any action that is needed.

Security information management products and concepts are good starting points for a discussion of security monitoring as a management strategy. The idea of security monitoring is more than a single product; it requires a conceptual shift in thinking about the role of information security in the organization. It is easy for an organization to purchase a product that handles the function of monitoring a variety of security information resources. It is more difficult to integrate that system in the policies and procedures of a large, complex organization. Taking all that information and formulating a response requires a change in the basic security management paradigm.

Monitoring vs. Auditing

The first required shift in thinking is to understand that security monitoring is not the same thing as security auditing. Chapter 14 is entirely devoted to the concepts of auditing security. Auditors take "snapshots" of organizations and report their findings based on what they found at that point in time. An audit report is valid only for the period of time that the auditor spent doing his research. Security monitoring in this context is not static; it is looking at events and information to create a real-time picture of security and to develop a plan to respond to the changes in the security profile. Testing security and security products has a similar approach; the results are important but of limited use in understanding what is going on in a company minute by minute.

Thus, both auditing and testing of security are approaches to documenting the status of security. A way to understand this is to look at the basic auditing model. The role of an auditor is that of an outside judge or expert. An auditor should not be involved in operational procedures in a hands-on way. An example is to have an audit of a security policy with respect to network operations. The policy may state that "all external network connectivity will go through a firewall and use a virtual private network (VPN) or through a challenge response system in the case of a dial-up connection." The auditor's role in this case is to verify if this is true through the analysis of network connections and the testing of the effectiveness of these protection mechanisms. A common problem that might be found is a new network connection that is not going though a firewall, or a wireless network that has not previously been identified. The auditor notes this exception to policy and reports it to management for corrective action. In an extreme case, the auditor might escalate his finding for immediate action if he believed that it posed significant risk to the business. That action might include shutting down the network connection or the immediate purchase and implementation of the appropriate control mechanism such as a firewall. Further suggestions of corrective action might include changes in the procedures that allowed the unapproved connection to be made in the first place.

Each of these actions is more or less static in nature. The auditor has a set of controls that are reviewed on either a periodic or somewhat random basis (surprise audit). The corrective actions are also somewhat static as they address written policies and procedures. The actions are not dynamic and only in extreme cases will an auditor recommend operational changes that should take place during the time of the audit. The net result of this is to reinforce the idea that audits are point controls, i.e., a control function that reports on status at a single point in time. The actual controls being audited can be stronger or weaker at any point before or after the audit. The auditor can only attest to the status of the control as it existed at the time of examination.

This is similar to the results from proactive testing of security by either the management of the security department or by consultants or other external professionals. Test security is similar in nature to the function of audit. The idea is to select a set of controls and design a testing regimen that will show the effectiveness of the controls. There are numerous types of tests for security controls, including:

- *Penetration tests.* These are attempts to access the network or other information system resources, such as servers, without proper authorization. There are several programs available to do this, including a number of shareware programs that are available for free over the Internet.
- *War dialing.* This is an attempt to gain access to either a voice or data network without authorization. The term comes from a 1980s movie, *War Games.* The intruder in this case is trying to gain access through an unsecured telephone line. Particularly at risk are PBXs and dial-up ports on servers.
- *Application controls.* Many software applications have their own security schemes that are part of the application design. These controls are mainly for controlling authorization levels of activity within the application. Testing in this case usually consists of taking an authorized user credential that has minimal authority and trying various combinations of transactions and activities to see if the authority can be exceeded without approval. The simple version of this is seeing if a user ID that has read-only authority can be used to execute a transaction or system function.

There are many more details involved in the testing process. A good test requires a plan, step-by-step activities, and documentation of all results along with an action plan if remedial action is needed. Testing should be done away from the production environment or at a time when it is offline so that the system will not be further compromised. In no case should the test include the movement of real money or the sending of confidential information outside of the corporate network.

A related topic in testing has to do with whom the business hires to perform the test. Some people propose the idea of hiring so-called ethical or "whitehat" hackers. Ethical hackers are consultants who will attempt to access the network or system using a variety of scripted attacks. Some of their methods are commonly used by auditors, but often they will do things that may border on being illegal activities. Many firms have prohibited the hiring of ethical hackers because they are concerned that the information gathered by the hacker may be used later in an illegal act. Sometimes the whitehat hacker is a former "blackhat" hacker who has actually engaged in unethical attacks on businesses.

The choice of whom to use to perform a test is up to management. The choices range from the Big Four audit firms, boutique security testing firms, or the independent ethical hacker. In any case, there should be a formal contract with the company or individual doing the testing. Privacy policies must also be part of the contract. That contract should have confidentiality language as well as strict liability statements to protect the business in the event that laws are broken as a result of the work of the consultant.

Most companies already have a wealth of information on the status of their security systems and do not believe they need another test or audit of their systems. All servers come with audit trails and have reporting tools on suspect activity. Likewise, firewalls have alert reports and audit logs. Virus scanners keep detailed information on the scans that have been performed and the results of those scans. These are good sources of information but, like auditing and testing, they do not provide a format for looking at the status of the security measures on a consolidated and real-time basis.

Activity Monitoring and Audit Trails

One of the goals of auditing is to document the status of the controls that are in place. Another goal is to provide management with information on compliance with regulations, industry standards, and best practices. This information can then be used to improve those controls over time. Sometimes that may mean changing the existing control settings; other times it may mean the necessity of implementing additional control mechanisms. The basic goal of auditing is designed to work directly with the basic duty of management to have an effective control program in place.

Audit reports and audit trails are good sources of information for the security manager; another source is activity-based information. There is a lot of data in audit reports and systems logs that record activity that may or may not be of interest to security staff. A good example is password reset information. On a given day, many users have to have their passwords reset. There are also other customer service-type requests to have user IDs issued or revoked. These activities act like background noise in a large room; each conversation is independent of the others and there is no way to understand all the conversations at once. That background noise, however, can cover up critical information. There is not necessarily anything wrong at a company that resets a hundred user passwords a day. But, what if one day there were a thousand passwords reset? What if the normal activity is to add 15 new users and delete a similar number, and then one day there were no requests for new users but 20 requests to delete users? Those events may be coming through authorized channels, but at the same time they may be indications of suspicious activity. If those reports were only reviewed periodically, that activity might go unnoticed for weeks or months. Those activities may pose a threat to the organization, but without a means to filter the information and identify which item is important, the threats will go unnoticed.

This is one way to view the idea of security monitoring; it is a way of looking at activity levels as a control, in addition to looking at the activity itself. Monitoring, as defined here, is the concept of a continuum of controls. In this approach, the controls are part of a larger process of continuous testing, reporting, and improvement. Here is how it works:

- Control systems report on activity in real time. The reporting consists of streams of information coming into a central point for analysis. The reported information most likely comes first from traditional sources such as audit trails and systems alerts and alarms.
- Activity logs also report on a real-time basis, but typically that information is collected for periodic review. Activity logs can be used to develop a baseline profile of the actions at a business, and then that information can be used together with the audit and alarm information to identify other weaknesses in the risk profile of a company.
- Ideally, configuration management information should also be monitored. For example, if a new server has come online, that information needs to be collected and reported to the security console. The server needs to have the appropriate controls in place; otherwise, it could create an exposure or threat to the business.
- A collection system picks up the information from all the control sources and combines it into a single view. Alert levels of various systems have to be rationalized so that they report on similar frequencies and levels of attention. A "high" alert level from one system must relate to a similar reporting level in another.
- The collection system reports on the status of security systems as well as the level of alerts. The system then has programs that look for related events.
- The security console then would be reviewed by a person who identifies the events that need further research or action.

These steps are generic to most monitoring systems that may already exist, such as physical security alarms. The difference for an information security system is that all controls would come to a central point and there is an attempt to look at threats from a more global perspective.

How Security Information Management Systems Work

There are three basic approaches to a security information management system:

1. Using existing tools that monitor information system resources and create a separate set of reports or a console for security information. Products such as OpenView from HP and Tivoli from IBM can be used in this manner. This approach makes effective use of existing

information paths, but it may lack the ability to deal with the diversity of security systems and their special reporting needs.

2. Consolidating information through product consoles. Some firewalls allow for the creation of a hierarchy of management consoles, creating a "manager of managers" arrangement. This does not solve the problem of consolidating firewall information with access control information, but it does help ease the management burden. A variation on this approach is the recent introduction of multi-function security appliances. These are systems that combine several security features under a single management system on a dedicated server. Some of these systems combine a firewall with an intrusion-detection system. Combining these systems helps the SIM process as it reduces the number of information sources that need to be monitored.

3. The third approach is to implement a formal SIM product. This is the most expensive approach as it requires specially designed systems that have a single function. It is conceptually the approach that fully addresses the problem, as it deals with both the system diversity issue and event correlation problems, and uses filters that are specifically designed for security management.

Today, most security departments still monitor devices independently and do not try to bring information together other than for generic management activity reporting. More and more firms, though, are seeing the need to gather this information and report to management on a timely basis, creating a growing market for these products as well as presenting additional information to management for review.

Other Security Information Monitoring Sources

The single-largest other source of information to monitor is physical access information. Some companies are using the same ID badges used for access control to their buildings as they do for sign-on to their networks and systems. Even if the badges are not used for systems access control, the information from the access control system can be useful to the security management console. The ability to say for certain that a person was on site when he used a system resource can be very helpful in doing forensic research on a policy violation. This also dovetails into the debate on having a Chief Information Security Officer (CISO) or a Chief Security Officer (CSO) at the top of the organization (see Chapter 3). The combination of all information sources can give a more complete risk profile than can be had when information is kept in organizational silos.

Other sources of information that can be useful to monitor include operating system performance statistics, file transfer and access information, and vendor-supplied information. The latter can be particularly important when vendors send alerts on system software patches that pertain to security. This information needs to go to the security team as well as to the technical and operational management teams responsible for server maintenance. The security team should track vendor updates and security alters and report on the status of the changes to the corporate servers.

File transfer information needs to be reviewed first as part of security policy. Any business relies on the electronic transfer of files between itself and business partners; thus file transfers *per se* cannot be prohibited. What can and should be restricted is how files are transferred and who can approve transfers. The FTP protocol is one that can be abused at the local level and is often restricted through the use of rules on the corporate firewall. Not all users need to be able to transfer files using FTP, while transferring certain file types as e-mail attachments may be a routine part of business. Certain file types may also be restricted as a part of policy, such as music files (MP3), and any violations of that policy should be reported to the security monitoring system.

Some vendors are also proposing a middle ground in this collection and monitoring of security information, i.e., the use of multi-function security appliances. Single-purpose firewalls are giving way to multi-function servers that have firewalls and intrusion-detection systems on the same device. The idea is that putting these devices together can reduce the cost of having separate devices on the network. The idea has two additional benefits: (1) to reduce the level of effort it takes to install and maintain the devices and (2) to link the reporting of alerts and alarms together to reduce the volume of information that needs to be monitored. One of the stated benefits of this approach is that these devices are built from the ground up as security systems and are not just another piece of software layered on top of a PC or server operating system. This is an emerging idea that has merit, but it also does not take away anything from the idea of security monitoring; if anything, it shows the merit of the idea and the effect it is having on the marketplace.

It is clear that there are a number of choices to be made as to the extent of monitoring that a SIM system can perform. Those choices are a part of the organizational choices made with respect to the role of information security within the business. Another area to discuss at this point is privacy and how privacy fits into security monitoring.

Privacy and Security Monitoring

Privacy is emerging as a separate discipline from security. Initially, information security and privacy were linked through the idea of user authorization. Once a user, whether a person or a system resource, has been authenticated, the next step is to see what level of authority the user has. The simplest version of this is to restrict authority to actions such as read, write, and update. This became more complex over time (read what? write what?). As systems grew to multiple-applications and multiple-users systems, it became obvious that there needed to be more restrictions, and the logical place to put those controls was in the security management software.

Privacy, as it has become a major management issue, has recently made authorization schemes more complex and more visible at the same time. Managing privacy now has a legal side that did not exist when it was part of the general duties of the security department. Knowing who has access to specific pieces of information and limiting access to only authorized personnel are among the privacy duties that overlap security administration.

Privacy has two issues with respect to security monitoring. The obvious one is that security monitoring assists in acting as a control on the protection of information from unauthorized access and disclosure. Security monitoring provides management with a way to quickly identify actions that may indicate breaches in security policy and to react quickly to close those holes. The other way that security monitoring assists privacy management is through the ability to assist in any investigation that may be necessary. Having all relevant information collected at a single point will make such investigation easier and faster.

Security monitoring is not a privacy control; it is just another option in the controls available to management. It cannot substitute for a properly designed and implemented authentication and authorization system. Monitoring is mainly a reactive system that is, at best, a detective control, but it is not a preventive control. A well-formed security program has components of all control types, protective, reactive, detective, and proactive.

Reactions to Security Monitoring Information

The basic premise behind auditing and testing is that all security controls deteriorate over time. The moment a control is put in place is when it is most effective. Once a control has been implemented, it can be changed, attacked, or avoided by someone. What happens then is a stair step back to the desired control level. For example, consider a scale of security, with 100 as being fully implemented and effective. Every time the security control is changed, it must be tested against that scale. If a user is granted an exception to policy, the effective rating of security will be less than 100. If a new network connection is made and it is not done in accordance with policy, the rating will be lower still. At some point, the security staff will notice these changes and bring the system back in compliance and the rating will return to 100, hence the stair-step graph of security effectiveness. The accompanying chart in Exhibit 1 shows this idea reflected in quarterly monitoring of the effectiveness of the controls for a firewall and for user ID

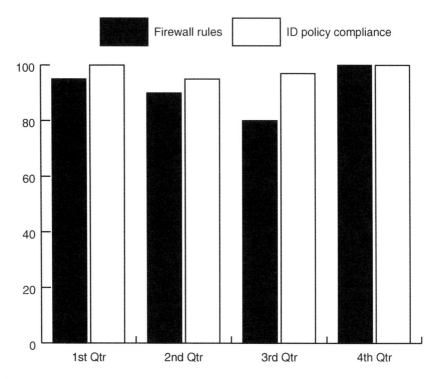

Exhibit 1. Stair-Step Chart of Security Level

policy compliance. Without monitoring and updating, the effectiveness will continue to deteriorate over time.

There are some management decisions that come with the idea of security monitoring. The first is to decide who is to do the monitoring and how they should report their findings. This is a two-pronged issue. The first part has to do with the management of the security console. The monitoring of this information can be passive or active. In a passive management model, the people monitoring the console are recording and reporting the information only, and they do not have authority to take action on their own. This is a similar approach that is taken with physical security monitoring. When an alarm is sounded, the console's job is to make sure the alarm is real and not an error. Other than that, the console's job is to escalate the alarm report for someone else to follow up and take action. An information security monitoring system can be managed in a similar manner. The person on the console can look to see that the reporting system is still up and running and beyond that he cannot take any independent action.

Another aspect is the reporting of security incidents. It does not matter who does the monitoring in this case, as the important thing is they report security incidents quickly. Security incidents, though, may be difficult to judge, which is why some companies that have implemented a security monitoring system have chosen to have people monitoring the console who have the ability and authority to take action independently. Their action may include shutting down a network node or revoking a user's ID credentials. That action can affect production operations and services, which is why such decisions should be made by senior management as part of the process of implementing a security monitoring system.

Other areas that require senior management input in the design and approval of a security monitoring system are the obvious ones of staffing and escalation. If a company already has a CSIRT in place, then the monitoring process needs to be interfaced with the function of the CSIRT to prevent duplication of effort. This is not difficult and is generally done through the documented escalation policy and procedures.

Other reporting issues should include routine performance reports to management. These would include documenting the number of incidents over time, type of incident, action taken, and any impact on business operations. These reports should roll up to executive management as part of business risk management and may even be reported to the appropriate board oversight committee.

Problems with Security Monitoring

Although the concept of security monitoring seems attractive and there is an increasing number of tools for doing so, the idea has yet to gain widescale acceptance. This may be due to a number of factors such as cost, perceived benefits, and even fear.

The cost of security monitoring is greater than the cost of the security tools and systems alone, which is an obvious statement. A security monitoring system will require either the purchase of software off the shelf or the modification of existing tools. The reports from the system will have to be looked at and actions taken or there is no benefit from the process. The console would require 24/7 monitoring. The previous discussion about management decisions over who manages the console come into play. The console could be placed in a network operations center and added to the duties of that center with all actions being the responsibility of the CSIRT or the on-call security contact, which would help lower the operating cost of the console. There would need to be training of all personnel, and the escalation policies would need to reflect the responsibilities of the network operations personnel as well as the security staff.

A more difficult issue has to do with identifying the benefits from security monitoring. The information that will be gathered through monitoring should lower the risk to the business through improved response and faster reaction to an incident; beyond that, the benefits are difficult to quantify. What is it worth to know that there have been additional policy violations? Proactive security can only be quantified in terms of potential loss through prevention. This is true about other risks, such as fire prevention. In the case of sprinkler systems and other fire detection and prevention measures, the benefit can only be clearly proven if a fire occurs. Even then, it could be questioned that the fire suppression equipment could not be cost justified unless an equally severe fire occurred in a similar facility without the same safeguards. Clearly, that is not practical and most senior managers are accustomed to looking at these decisions from a more practical point of view.

There are more realistic and practical problems to discuss about security monitoring, mainly with a false-positive and information overflow. The false-positives are a familiar part of the reporting that come from security systems today, and security professionals are accustomed to dealing with that issue. That is why there needs to be a clearly documented escalation policy and plan. A typical complaint from the use of intrusion-detection systems (a proven technology) is that they produce too many false-positives, forcing the security team to chase shadows instead of being able to concentrate on real problems.

The problem of information overflow is a little more serious. The amount of information that will come into a security console can be overwhelming. The use of intelligent software agents for gathering console information (mentioned earlier) is one way to deal with this problem. The other way has to do with the initial setup of the console system. In almost every case, there needs to be a period of time in the project plan to review the reports coming out of the system and adjust them accordingly. In reality, that is a normal part of project management and should not be a major decision criterion for implementing a security monitoring system.

There are some additional technical issues that will come up as part of the project, including the disparate nature of the reporting systems and their alert and alarm levels. The security monitoring software should reflect the nature of the information technology infrastructure where it will be used. This is again a rather basic project management issue that applies to any technology purchase.

Senior Management Issues and Security Monitoring

Most of the critical issues for senior management have been discussed in other areas of this chapter. Security monitoring is not an endpoint, but part of the overall strategic plan for security in a business. As part of that plan, the costs and benefits of monitoring need to be included in the decision process.

Once the decision has been made to implement a monitoring process, the remaining decisions, though important, are largely operational in nature. Who will do the monitoring, the staffing level for the monitoring process, the skill of those people, and their authority to react to incidents are all decisions that need to be made as part of the project plan. There should be an ongoing evaluation of the monitoring process and regular reviews of the staffing levels as well as reports on security incidents.

Monitoring security in this way can have some benefits in the short run, but it is in the long run that this will likely have the largest payoff. As businesses become more and more dependent on their IT infrastructure and in doing business across the Internet, the risks from security incidents will grow greater and greater. There is no way to reduce those risks to zero, and the only practical solution is through a combination of preventive and reactive measures. A well-designed security monitoring system can be an effective part of the overall strategy for risk reduction.

Chapter 14
Auditing and Testing a Strategic Control Process

Introduction: The Role of Auditing and Testing

The role of the auditor in an organization is subject to confusion by many people in business. A common misconception is that auditing is a substitute for other management control processes. Likewise, other people believe that the presence of an external auditor eliminates the need for policies and other internal controls. Neither of these is true as the auditor plays a unique role in business that is not a substitute for other controls, but is an entirely separate discipline.

In a similar way, testing, particularly the testing and review of security policies, is also sometimes thought of as a control in and of itself. The reality is that auditing of the control process is similar to testing those same processes. Absence of a control means there is nothing to be audited or tested. The absence of a control robs the testing of any use in measuring the strength or weakness of a management control. It is important that the executives responsible for a business understand how auditing and testing fit into the control process and what role management plays in that same realm.

Auditing is best thought of as a measurement of the effectiveness and accuracy of a management control at a point in time by a third party, which means that (1) there has to be a control to measure, (2) the control has to be documented so that it can be tested against a standard, and (3) the control is effective and is being used as designed. The results of the audit examination report the facts based on the point in time that the audit was conducted. Auditors have recently made efforts to make their examinations more reflective of the volatility that exists in today's business environment. The Federal Reserve Bank now conducts "continuous" audits of major banks and financial institutions. Instead of coming in on an annual basis and taking a "snapshot," the Fed has a resident auditor on site at the bank or financial institution that continually works with it on its controls and control processes.

The point about a third party conducting the audit is where the difference between auditing and testing first becomes apparent. Testing, in the context of information security, is a process done usually by the owner of a control to measure the effectiveness of the control. Testing can be done either by the owner of the process or by a trusted third party. Testing is an important part of the management process and, although it can be more rigorous than an audit, it also is usually seen as lacking the independence that comes from a third-party review. Even when management hires an outside party to perform testing, it is usually under the direction of management and at its request. The control of the process can cloud the objectivity and make the results suspect.

A common concept for both auditing and testing is the issue of time. In Chapter 13 on security monitoring, the issue of time and changes to the environment are discussed in greater detail. Time affects everything about an audit. Was the control in place at the time the audit occurred? Are errors or alarms that come from the control reported in a timely manner? Do the controls themselves get reviewed on a routine basis to ensure their effectiveness? Finally, was the report from the auditor also made on a timely basis to ensure that any problems could be corrected before any harm was done? These are important parts of the audit process and the audit report that goes to management. The final part of the audit process is the response from management and it, too, is time based, as management is expected to respond quickly to any deficiencies that are found and to resolve them as soon as practical.

Auditing and Security Management

One of the humorous comments that many information security professionals make is that they are not the most disliked people in the company; instead, that distinction goes to their only friend in the organization — the auditor. The two roles are connected as they both perform a control function, but the important thing to remember is that the auditor is independent and the information security area will also be audited.

That still leaves the two areas to find a way to work together to achieve some common goals. The two roles are complementary for the most part and should rarely be placed in an adversarial position, which does happen from time to time, particularly with the different view the two have over the design of a control.

With regard to the design of controls, the auditor does not want to approve a control ahead of time as there is a fear of compromising his independence. If the auditor reviews and approves the control before it is put in place and later criticizes it in an audit (the thinking goes), then the audited person can claim that he was only doing what the auditor had requested or otherwise agreed to. Auditors protect their independence and work diligently to ensure that none of their actions could compromise their position as an outsider looking in at management.

There is another level to the roles of security and audit and that comes from the role of external auditors. There are two major types of external auditors — third-party auditors performing annual reviews and audit staff from oversight or regulatory bodies. The first group in the United States includes the familiar names of the Big Four audit firms: Pricewaterhouse-Coopers, Deloitte, KPMG, and Ernst & Young. The other group is usually related to either governmental bodies (Federal Reserve, FDIC, etc.) or industry associations. In either case, they play a similar role in that they use industry standards and report their findings to an oversight agency that has the power to bring the target company into compliance.

The degree of external review has greatly increased recently with the scandals that have come to light in publicly traded companies. Those scandals have led to the creation of a new law, the Sarbanes–Oxley Act, which increased the importance and visibility of the role of the audit committee. Prior to Sarbanes–Oxley, management could refuse to agree to an audit issue raised by both internal and external auditors and make their feelings known to the Audit Committee with little fear of being overruled. Now management must sign off to the board and the shareholders on these issues and be personally accountable for these compliance issues. That has greatly raised the stakes with respect to audit reports and audit responses, and it also has made the whole audit process much more transparent to the public.

Security Audits

One way to look at the role of the auditor in information security is through the information sources he has at his disposal. On the one hand is the field work from audits into systems controls and processes; on the other hand there is the information available from audit trails and audit records. The latter has a great deal of information and overlap with the other security control functions and will be examined first.

Audit trails are records that are created to track system activities and processes for further analysis. They form the basis of standard business control practices and serve as an information source for a variety of activities. The major uses for these include problem identification, investigation, controls monitoring, and policy enforcement. As a result, one of the important areas where audit and security overlap is the maintaining of the integrity of the audit records. It is up to the information security administrator to ensure that the audit files cannot be modified or read by unauthorized personnel. It is up to security, working with the auditor, to design those protection schemes and ensure that they are properly functioning. Loss of the integrity of audit reports and audit trails is an embarrassing problem for management that may even have legal or regulatory implications.

Information Protection

In the creation of a robust information security program, there are a host of policy alternatives that are reviewed in earlier chapters. Some of these key issues have been discussed such as information ownership (Chapter 5) and authentication schemes (Chapter 9). In one sense, those two ideas come together with the concept of security labels and information classification.

One of the ways that information protection is managed is through the use of security labels and authorization models. Labels in this context are the traditional and well-known security labels of Public, Classified, Secret, and Top Secret. Most organizations have at least a rudimentary use of labels. Many materials are marked "confidential" or "for internal use only." In other cases, through the use of authentication systems, access to computer networks and applications is restricted to employees or customers. Information can be further restricted by using more granular access control models, forming the basis of a need-to-know access scheme. This is the basis of the concept of authorization, which is the next step beyond authentication.

There are two basic models for authorization, which are done as part of the access control scheme:

1. *Bell-LaPadula.* This model is based on the need-to-know concept of access and states that an entity (user or computer resource) cannot read information that has a higher label. Someone with "Public" access cannot read "Secret" information. On the other hand, the rule in this model also says that the user cannot write to a lower level of sensitivity.
2. *Biba.* This model is almost the inverse of the Bell-LaPadula model. In this case, the entity cannot read information with a lower label and cannot write to a higher level.

The reason to discuss these models is to explain conceptually how audit trails work and how they maintain their integrity. In the Bell-LaPadula model, the audit trail would have a label that provides a high level of security; all information would flow up and could be written to an audit log but not be read. That may seem hard to understand at first, but it makes sense. To have value, the audit log must be a complete record of activity, and a program that is designed to write to the log would have the authority to write log records but would not need to read them. The only entities with authority to read the records would be those with the highest security clearance, such as the auditors. In the Biba model, you reverse the information flow and use the same concept.

The important thing for management to learn from these concepts is that a properly designed information processing system can be written to capture all relevant transaction information while limiting access to reading that information to those with a real need to know.

There are a number of good places to find detailed information on auditing and how auditors do their job. Control Objectives for Information and Related Technology (CobIT) is a document available from ISACA, the Information Security and Audit and Control Association (www.isaca.org). It provides information on over 300 control objectives related to information security. The CobIT also does a good job of explaining the roles of management and auditing. It stresses the fact that it is up to management to ensure that there are appropriate control systems in place that work in concert with business objectives. There is also a lot of effort made to ensure that the auditors also understand that their role is to support management in its objective of creating a satisfactory controls environment. In that way, Auditing is a strategic partner in the business with management, but auditors also understand the importance of maintaining their independence and providing a separate voice to management regarding controls and practices.

The FFIEC (Federal Financial Institutions Examination Council, www.ffiec.gov) also has a wealth of public information available that deals with auditing and control objectives at banks and financial institutions. The FFIEC acts as a clearinghouse for the regulatory agencies that oversee the banking industry in the United States. By looking though this information, the senior executive can gain insight into the concepts behind system controls and the objectives for auditing and testing systems. This is important and any conflict between the development staff and the auditors or security staff will pit functionality against control objectives. Senior management is often called in to arbitrate those disputes and it is helpful if they understand the objective and goals of each side. Many senior managers, however, have a good understanding of the goals of the business managers, but lack a background in the basic concept of audit and security controls.

Audit Logs and Audit Trails

The first time many executives see an audit log is after there has been a problem and the information in the audit trail is part of the documentation after the fact. Most executives and managers at the top level of a company are more familiar with an audit report, as they see those as part of their routine job functions.

The information written to audit logs is generally similar across all types of information systems. It consists of a time and date stamp, identification of the creator of the record, source and routing information, and the details of the record itself. The audit record is usually a mirror of a routine transaction with the other information added to it to make it serve its designed purpose. The audit trail typically is not actively monitored and its main use is research after the fact. Some audit trails also have alarm thresholds where there are activity levels that trigger additional steps on top of event tracking. These are very useful in alerting management to suspicious activity, and the information in the audit trail is the primary source of information in the investigation of the suspicious activity.

This dual use of audit logs is a good example of why there is often confusion over the role of the auditor. The fact that audit information has a dual use does not compromise the independence of the auditor; it instead serves to reinforce his role in the management controls process. Audit logs are not the only information source that the auditor uses and, in fact, much of the information needed to conduct an audit is dual-use information. Auditors also will use network maps, network testing tools, activity logs from authentication systems, logs from change management systems, and transaction sampling reports as part of their information-gathering process. Many of these reports and systems are the same ones that a system developer will use as part of the project management process.

This is the point where testing and auditing come together again. A lot of tools that are used for testing security on a proactive basis are useful for auditors in their testing of the controls systems.

Security Testing and Analysis

When security testing is discussed, there are several different areas under discussion. One is the testing of internal business applications for integrity and functionality. Another is the testing of the control systems protecting the IT infrastructure. These both fall into the category of testing, but they have different goals and use different tools.

Looking at testing and its role in the system development life cycle, security functionality needs to be part of the design process, and then those components need to be included in the testing phase of the project. Testing in the system development life cycle falls into the traditional categories of unit test, system test, certification test, and integration testing. In many cases, the security team will write up its testing criteria and the actual testing will be done by the development staff. The test results will be reviewed by the security staff and they will get to sign off on them. This holds true for both in-house and custom applications as well as for commercial off-the-shelf systems (COTS). In the case of COTS software and hardware, the vendor certification of the security functionality should be used as part of the acquisition process, but should not be allowed to sub-stitute for testing done by the security team.

The argument for independent testing of applications is one that is made frequently during the system acquisition and implementation process. Many managers have questioned the need to test a COTS system, under the assumption that any problems in the system would have already been discovered by other users. This is not always a safe assumption as each user of an information system may have slightly different needs and uses that can expose previously unknown problems. A multi-billion dollar bank in the southeast United States recently purchased a new financial transaction processing system from a reputable vendor. During the system test phase, certain transactions were entered that crossed company lines. The system design should have prevented the entry of transactions that were outside the boundaries of one company, but did not do so. As a result, the bank ended up delaying the project several weeks while the vendor made changes that reinforced the organizational integrity of the data entry system. That is the type of problem that testing is designed to find before a system is moved into production. In this case, the failure of the system would be desired as the result of a successful testing plan.

This also helps to understand the strategic importance of the goals of Microsoft's Trustworthy Computing Initiative: "security by design, security by default, and secure in deployment." In the case of this bank, the system, which was not a Microsoft product, failed in all three aspects. The idea of making security a strategic goal will help prevent occurrences such as this in the future.

Application Controls and Strategic Security Goals

The controls in financial applications systems are generally designed with secure operations in mind. Most systems that deal with money come with a standard set of features addressing common goals such as separation of duties and variable levels of authority (person A can approve a transaction within a limit of $X to $Y). This is familiar territory and often this type of control would be assumed rather than detailed in the product specification.

What is important to remember is that the auditor and the security staff will not assume that these rules exist and will instead want to test their effectiveness. If the system fails these tests it should be within the authority of the security staff to act like the bank mentioned earlier and refuse to allow the system to be moved into production. Time for testing should be part of the project plan, and the project manager must be made aware of that fact and held accountable so that it is not skipped if the project falls behind schedule.

An alternative to the controls within the application is the controls in the operating system, the network management system, and other higher-level applications. Those controls are generally better suited for identity management and access control and typically lack the granularity needed for financial applications. There are some systems that work in concert, however, with the application control systems. Strong authentication systems such as biometrics or public key infrastructure are useful in ensuring the identity of a person or entity performing a high-risk transaction. Likewise, digital certificates are useful in preventing fraud and encryption systems will help prevent message tampering or modification. All of those are part of a robust controls infrastructure and are not intended to be used alone in most application settings; rather they are intended to be part of a larger controls infrastructure. The internal controls process of a well-designed application will provide the incremental controls needed to complete that process.

The intersection of applications controls and operating systems controls is one that needs to be well thought out as part of the security strategy of the business. In some cases, for low-value applications, it is possible to rely on nonapplication system-level controls. Most firms do so with respect to office productivity applications such as word processing and spreadsheet systems. In this case, the user would sign onto the network and be authenticated and then have access to common applications. Access to the next level of applications such as e-mail usually requires further authentication services, and access to business applications such as accounting systems may have another set of controls. This complexity is what drives interest into single sign-on systems (see Chapter 10) and adds to the difficulty for auditors to ensure the integrity of the processing systems and for them to test the appropriate controls in these systems.

The related topic to discuss is the testing of these complex relationships. Security holes may inadvertently be opened with the addition of new applications and processes to a secured environment. When any system is added or there are changes to functionality, it is very important to take a structured look at how those changes affect the control systems that are in place. There is often a conflict between the development team and the controls areas (auditing and security) at this point, as the developers are trying to stay on budget and may resist the additional testing requirements, saying they are outside the scope of the project. Management should have testing requirements in place as part of the project management system that ensure this does not get overlooked. If there is a conflict it will be up to both the project sponsor and the executive in charge of the controls process to negotiate and resolve the issue. Each of these managers has a goal that may initially conflict with the other's, as the application owner wants the benefits of the new software and the security manager wants to ensure that the new system does not change the overall risk profile of the business. Resolving this conflict is one of the roles that the senior executive has to play as part of his responsibilities. The resolution of conflicts like this should not be left to the project manager alone as he may take the easy route and avoid doing the incremental testing.

Results from tests as well as problems that are reported by users and customers are another challenging area for management. Although it is easy to say that the company welcomes reports of problems, it is something else entirely to make sure that there is a process in place to deal with those reports once they are made.

Reporting of Security Problems and the Role of the Auditor

There is a debate even among security professionals about the best way to handle reports on security exposures and breaches. One side in this issue believes that all incidents should be reported quickly and openly in order for them to receive the proper attention. People with this view think that the best way to protect their systems and assets is to have the full support and cooperation of their user community. They welcome all reports and emphasize that weaknesses do not constitute as great a vulnerability to the company as do unknown exposures.

Another group in this debate believes equally strongly that all reports of security issues must be investigated prior to their being made public. People with this view are worried about erroneous reports as well as the possibility that publicizing a weakness will encourage people to exploit that weakness. These people may also be believers in the idea of "security by obscurity," where the less everyone knows, the safer things are.

This is a philosophical debate that should have the involvement of executive management in the final decision. It is up to the executive team to decide which is a greater risk, the known or the unknown. Auditing can play a valuable role in this discussion by focusing on the real issues and not on scare tactics. Auditors understand how to discuss their findings in practical business terms and how to rate the severity of weaknesses and exposures. It is their job, after all, to protect the business through testing those controls and evaluating their effectives. That is why they may be the best place to go to understand this issue and may help in making an informed decision.

The major decision hierarchy for disclosing security problems is if the problem is with a product owned by the business or if it is used by the business. Although the paths are related, they have some major differences that management needs to be aware of before making any decisions.

If the security problem is within the company or one of its own products, the issues that management needs to think about are:

- *Damage to the company if the exposure is not disclosed and corrected.* Sometimes closing a hole will mean shutting down parts of a Web site or a business application. In those cases, a message needs to be crafted that explains the outage, in addition to assessing the problem, looking at the correction alternatives, and implementing the appropriate one.
- *The reputation of the company is also at risk if the disclosure issues are not properly handled.* This is true whether it is a business-to-business (B2B) site or a business-to-customer (B2C) site; if the disclosure is not handled the right way, customers may lose confidence and decide to go elsewhere.
- *Timing of the announcement is very important.* Early disclosure may sound like a good tactic, but will only work if the information is correct. Making one announcement followed by a series of corrections and additions may cause more problems than would have occurred if the company had waited until it had all its answers.

It the company discovers a problem with someone else's software or products, there are also disclosure issues to consider. There is a general protocol that has emerged over the years for disclosing security vulnerabilities: first notify the vendor and see if there is an answer to the problem. If the vendor cannot solve it immediately, the next step is to see how long it will take to have a fix or a work-around prior to public disclosure. Most security experts agree with the process, even if it delays the public announcement for several days. The reason is a security vulnerability that is found may be known only to a few people, and announcing it before the vendor has a fix or patch can create a vulnerability for everyone who uses that product. Many companies do not immediately install the software patches announced by vendors. It is not uncommon for companies to wait 30 days or longer before installing a patch, especially if the threat to their environment is low. Announcing a vulnerability to the public exposes everyone who uses that product to that threat.

Auditors should not only be involved in the testing of security systems and procedures, they should also be part of the correction process. Many auditors stop their involvement once a response to their findings has been written and accepted by management. The auditor may feel that his independence would be compromised if he became too involved in the correction process; as a result he will not approve a solution, only offer an opinion that it addresses the problem he identified. This can be frustrating for management in the best of circumstances. Managers like certainty in their decisions. The more assistance the auditor can provide to ensure that a problem of exposure is being properly addressed, the better the solution will be received.

This goes directly to the next management issue, which is the mitigation of risks and exposures that are found either through an audit or in testing. In the case of testing, the correction cycle should be part of the systems development life cycle, so there should be a mechanism in place for tracking and correcting errors. Security exposures should be treated in the same way as other problems: they should be clearly identified, a mitigation strategy developed, and the correction made and retested.

Exposures uncovered by auditors should also be tracked. The plans should be approved by the relevant management area, and the implementation plan should be tracked and reported to management to ensure timely completion. Auditors generally assist in this process in that they will rate the severity of the problem and work with management on the timing of the corrective action. In most cases, there will also be an allowance for measuring the cost of corrective actions so that management can decide whether to accept the risk of leaving the exposure uncorrected or whether it is cost-effective to fix.

Auditing, Testing, and Strategic Security

When executive management is working in a strategic mode on security or any issue, the roles of each member of the team are an important part of the process. Understanding how auditing and testing fit into the business and how those functions fit into the security strategic plan is very important. Executive management needs to be fully involved in these processes and should not just say it has been delegated without checking further.

A fully developed systems development and project methodology will include clearly defined tasks for testing of applications and applications functionality. Those methodologies also need to include plans for testing security features and functionality in conjunction with the work of the security staff. The security staff alone should not be the only ones charged with seeing that security functions work as designed and that they meet the needs of the business.

Auditing also needs to work with management to make sure their plans meet the needs of the business. External auditors and regulators meet with the executive team to plan out their activities for the coming year and discuss any changes in the business that will affect their plans. That meeting has to be very open and the results have to be satisfactory to both parties. Auditors should not feel that their objectivity is compromised when they go to management to discuss their plans and activities. Likewise, management should not arbitrarily attempt to change the plans of auditors unless there are mitigating circumstances or, in some very unusual case, where the activity of the auditor may interfere with valid business functions (for example, a surprise audit in the middle of a major system conversion). There should be teamwork between the audit staff and the security staff as well as between the general auditors and the executives. Teamwork does not compromise integrity; it should be a way to make the results more accurate and relevant to the goals of the business. As set forth in the introduction to this chapter, the associations that support auditing stress the different roles of audit and management. Management and the audit staff should work in concert to make sure that the business controls are accurate and the results shown are correct and fair representations of the actions that have occurred.

Chapter 15
Outsourcing Security: Strategic Management Issues

Information Security Operations and Security Management

Beyond the discussions about technology, threats, and risks there is an operational side to information security that often gets overlooked by senior management. Particularly the administrative side of security management can be viewed as any other operational function in a business; there are customers, services, and costs that have to be managed. From the perspective of the Director of Information Security, most of these functions are assumed to be part of the job and, for the most part, the least interesting part. Information security professionals are generally more comfortable discussing encryption choices than they are staffing policies for their customer support operation. As a result, these administrative roles often are overlooked until there is a crisis that brings these management issues to the forefront.

In the chapters on authentication and single sign-on, much of the discussion was focused on the policy aspects of security and on the technical issues regarding the implementation of protection mechanisms. This is the normal view of security, that it is in almost equal parts a policy issue and a technical one. Information security professionals focus their attention on those two areas and there is very little discussion in professional literature on the operational aspects of security management. Security magazines and training courses do not offer much insight into administrative management or cost control objectives.

This is equally true in looking at some of the other technical solutions for security such as anti-virus programs, firewalls, and intrusion-detection systems. In any independent review and rating of the products in those markets, there is a great deal of information on the technical aspects of the products. There are tests done in labs that measure throughput, detection rates, and how easy or difficult it is to deploy the product in the field. There is rarely a discussion about the level of effort to maintain the product once it is deployed or how much effort is needed to administer the system in a typical environment. Security projects are similar in nature to any other project; there is a cost to implement security tools and there are ongoing costs for administration and maintenance that need to be examined and factored into the tactical and strategic plans of the business.

In the same light, there are decisions to be made about the management of the operations associated with security functionality. This is true for both physical security and information security, making this an issue for the Chief Information Security Officer (CISO) or Chief Security Officer (CSO) in the organization. These decisions start even higher in the organization with the decision about the amount of resources that will be dedicated to security. This is where the real commitment to security can be measured — how much the company will pay for security in both capital costs and operating costs. Once that decision is made, there are many related decisions about ways to optimize those expenses.

Throughout all aspects of business today there is ongoing discussion about what is the correct mix of expenses and how to optimize the return on investment. Using outside services has become a standard part of this equation in business. Where, in the past, most business were vertically integrated, more and more they are becoming specialized and they are looking for ways to move scarce resources to places where the return on investment is the greatest. One way to do this is to move low-value operations outside the company. This is a complex decision at best, and when it involves security it can be even more complicated.

Security functions are almost always thought of as cost centers. Security operational expenses are generally bundled into overhead and are thought of as part of the cost of doing business. As such, there will always be an interest in driving down those costs. One way to do so is to look at security as another operational area that has functions that can be done independently. Breaking down those tasks into components allows management to look for the low-cost way to provide each component service or function. One of the alternatives to providing functionality may be to look at which tasks can be done by a third-party service provider and which must be done by in-house personnel.

Management Issues Regarding the Outsourcing Decision

The initial decision to outsource a function is cost based. Companies believe they will achieve lower costs by moving operations such as payroll, physical security, cleaning services, and other functions to outside service providers. In many industries, the help desk has been outsourced even to other countries that provide sources of cheap labor. Some high-tech firms now rely on India as a supplier of programming resources for development or support work on software products. Higher-value operations such as information technology are becoming outsourcing targets at more and more companies. Network management and operations is also a popular area to move to a third party.

In the realm of information security, there have been a number of functions that have been targeted for management by third parties. Sometimes this has been as simple as the issuing of security tokens or the management or remote access systems. Other times, this has included network security and system auditing. A common term for outsourcing of information security operational functions is "managed security," which generally describes the management of firewalls, intrusion-detection systems, and anti-virus products.

The term "managed security," used by the security outsourcing industry, has certain assumptions that go with it. It implies that the service provider is more than an operational function; it adds value to the work that is performed. Another way to think about this is managed security vs. managing security. In the managed security option, certain distinct security functions are moved out of the business to a service provider, that, it is thought, can provide those services at a lower cost and also bundle some expertise that the client company does not have in house. The phrase "managing security" can be used to describe the oversight functions that will still need to be done at the client business. Managing security includes a mix of internal work and external services that are performed under the guidelines set forth in the security policy and procedures of the client firm. This extends the idea of security outsourcing away from just a cost decision and makes it part of the overall security architecture.

The initial goal of most outsourcing projects is to gain control of costs and lower them wherever possible. For many businesses, information technology is a means to an end, and the expertise in the business lies in products that are supported by IT rather than the technology itself. In those businesses, there are frequent concerns about the ability to stay current with technology and how to do so when the real expertise in the company lies elsewhere. Some of the benefits from outsourcing in these cases include:

- *Standardization of hardware and software.* By using a third-party provider, there usually are fewer exceptions to policies governing which products are the company standards. The service provider agreement usually will not cover technologies that are outside a standard list, giving them more power to limit policy exceptions.
- *Control and predictability of upgrade cycles.* Along with standardized products usually comes a schedule for upgrade cycles. This part of the contract may also include both the frequency of replacements (PCs will be replaced every three years, for example) and what

hardware and software may be used between upgrade cycles for new hires.

- *Support.* The support requirements in an outsourcing agreement may be the most difficult to manage. Standard response times are generally listed as well as a cost for emergency calls or if calls are more frequent than predicted in the preliminary agreement. The benefit to the business comes from having a standardized support plan across the enterprise. This means that the service levels should improve as a whole as the outsourcing company will apply standards for "break and fix," as well as for any routine service calls. This may mean that, in some cases, service will deteriorate if that area has special service above and beyond what has been the standard level.

That leads to the statement that using an outside service provider for anything requires an understanding of service levels and service measures. The service provider makes money through carefully managing its service levels and limiting its effort to whatever is specified in the contract; that is all a service provider is obligated to provide. As a result, it is critical to the success of an outsourcing project to understand all elements of the service to be provided and what tasks will continue to be done using internal resources. Prior to signing a contract, management needs to have its current service-level metrics studied and get buy-in from the areas that will use the service provider so that the contracted levels are adequate to meet their needs.

Another important management issue is quality assurance. One of the common refrains of managers explaining why some functions should not be outsourced is "we can do a better job ourselves." This may or may not be true, and the only way to know is to have the quality assurance metrics done and routinely monitored. Some of these are well-known issues such as the amount of downtime that is acceptable, input errors and correction rates, response time, repair time, and activity volumes and measures. Management should have these done prior to writing a contract and should understand any trending data that might be available on current performance measures.

There are many other management issues that should be included in a review of an outsourcing proposal, including protecting the privacy of information, custodial control of records in case there is an investigation of suspicious activity, and responses to legal inquiries. The customer of the outsourcing company has to have confidence that the service provider will protect his privacy and only respond to legal requests for information. The information in this case really belongs to the customer, not the service provider. The service provider should understand that there is a custodial responsibility for the data it is processing. In a custodial relationship, the true owner of the information is the one who has a right to control access, the information owner; that, in this case, is the organization that signed the outsourcing agreement. Chapter 5 (Establishing Information Ownership) has a good explanation of the difference in these roles and why it is important to keep them separate.

The legal issues regarding custodial relationships are becoming more complicated for business today. This is becoming a larger issue with the creation of the Department of Homeland Security and requests for information from that department and the Department of Justice. The Patriot Act of 2001 has some provisions in it that allow the U.S. government to request information without going to court for a subpoena. This has become an extremely controversial subject, and many business and civil libertarians are challenging those provisions in the Patriot Act. For executive management, these legal arguments add to the complexity of the outsourcing decision.

Outsourced Security Alternatives

Understanding service levels and performance metrics is a starting point to the outsourcing decision. This information can be combined with cost information and audit reports to create a picture of what areas management may see as viable for an outsourcing agreement. There are a number of areas in security that are good targets for outsourcing and they have some common characteristics:

- Clearly defined performance targets
- A high level of routine tasks or functions
- Little value added from the use of internal resources to perform the same task

As mentioned at the outset of this chapter, one of the terms used in the security press for outsourced security is "managed security." Using this term helps to delineate which security functions may be good candidates for the outsourcing process. In looking at the life cycle of a security program (see Chapter 2), there are different phases in its development and growth. In the early phases, the security program is often just an added responsibility for the network operations center or for the data center operations staff. In these cases, security is a task that may lack a full set of management processes. As the program matures, so does the need to better understand the security model that the firm wants, and there is a need to have round-the-clock security monitoring by trained staff. Those needs may be problematic due to cost issues, and the idea of managed security becomes an attractive alternative.

Managed security does not yet have a single common definition in the security industry. There are many functional areas that can be considered possible targets for outsourcing. This list is growing as more and more firms are entering this market space.

Common security functions that can be outsourced include the following:

- *Firewall installation, maintenance, and monitoring.* The service levels to be monitored here include uptime, repair time, and reaction time for change requests and the response plan for any security breaches.
- *Intrusion-detection systems (IDSs).* Service levels here are similar to those for firewalls, including uptime, repair time, and change in management. The critical one is the response to alerts and alarms. In the case of an IDS, responses may include shutting down a network node or rerouting traffic. Management must be fully aware of the response plan in the contract and should understand the implications of that plan.
- *Anti-virus systems and e-mail filtering* can be done remotely through a third party. The advantage is in getting virus signatures faster, reducing the chances of infection.
- *Voice system security.* PBXs and voice mail systems have a security exposure that can be caused and addressed by remote maintenance. Securing the maintenance ports of a voice system is an important security policy. Allowing remote management of the system may aid in monitoring the system for attacks by hackers as well as looking for patterns of fraudulent activity.
- *Identity management.* This includes setting up new users IDs, revoking IDs, changing authority levels, resetting passwords, and other forms of administration. Also included here is remote access administration as well as managing tokens or access cards.
- *Public key infrastructure (PKI) and digital certificates.* If a company has chosen digital certificates or PKI as part of its authentication scheme, it may use an outside company to manage key distribution, security tokens, and certificates. This can be an otherwise costly operation, and the pricing should be reviewed thoroughly prior to implementation. Creation of a PKI also requires high levels of security in the operational area, and that also means a high cost. There are several companies competing in both the PKI and the digital certificate marketplaces and they all describe themselves as a means of offering high-security alternatives at a lower cost.
- *Security monitoring and alerting.* As part of managing firewalls and intrusion-detection systems, some vendors will also perform centralized monitoring of those devices and combine that with other security systems such as anti-virus and virtual private networks.
- *Virtual private networks (VPNs) and remote access.* The idea of having a higher standard for remote access to corporate networks and computers is not new. The risk of unauthorized access increases when the network traverses public networks. As a result, companies

have turned to devices that provide stronger authentication than conventional user ID and PIN combinations. Managing the requests for remote access, issuing credentials, and monitoring the use of the remote access devices can be done using a third-party service, frequently provided by the networking companies themselves.

- *Incident response services.* Although a full-fledged Computer Security Incident Response Team (CSIRT, see Chapter 11) is an unlikely candidate for outsourcing, the investigations in support of those teams may be a better choice. A CSIRT usually needs to be a core part of IT management functionality, and it would be hard to find an effective way to have that done by a third party. That would require the third party to have a great deal of access and authority and might create more risk than it would reduce. On the other hand, computer forensics investigations do not occur as frequently and do require a high degree of specialized knowledge. The investigation into a security incident therefore becomes an obvious target to outsource to an external auditor or another expert firm. This can be done either through a standby contract with a firm or on an as-needed basis. The latter might require the payment of a retainer with the benefit of a promise of resource availability in case of an incident.

These functions can be offered as stand-alone services or may be bundled into other services offered to a business. One of the most common ways this is done is to bundle firewall and intrusion-detection monitoring with Web hosting and other ISP (Internet service provider) offerings. This may complicate the job of calculating the costs and benefits from outsourcing as these services will be bundled into a bottom-line price and not disclosed as separate line items in a contract. It is up to management to make sure that all services are clearly listed in contracts and each component is disclosed so that it can be examined and the correct measurement metrics included as part of the contract negotiations. It is also up to management to ensure that service levels are clearly stipulated in a contract and that they meet the needs of the client.

Understanding costs and contract components are just part of the analysis needed prior to moving services to a third party for management. There is a lot of work that goes into the analysis of the costs and benefits from outsourcing, and this starts with trying to calculate a return on investment.

Return on Investment (ROI) with Outsourced Services

This is a great debate in the study of outsourcing about the importance of calculating a return on investment (ROI) and how to use that information in the decision-making process. Carolyn D. Wylder, PE, former Deputy General Manager with the Metropolitan Atlanta Rapid Transit Authority

(MARTA), has participated in numerous studies on outsourcing of various business services. Now with David Evans and Associates, a Portland, Oregon, general engineering firm, she says that her experience is that cost should not be the driving factor in an outsourcing decision. While it is possible to calculate an ROI, she believes the more important issue is the ability to reallocate scarce resources to more important activities. Every business has high-value and low-value operations. Executive management has many demands on its time, and reviewing the activities of low-value operations should not be one of them if possible. This is true for management of any business and information technology operations and functions should not be an exception.

The ROI proponents base their analysis on before-and-after pictures of the activity under study. They use a predecision-activity cost model along with the volume metrics that must be gathered on the activity to build a cost model. For information security activities, the costs in most cases that are the highest in this approach are those that have to do with labor-intensive activities such as user ID administration, password resets, and token or certificate management in advanced authentication systems. These are also low-value activities for a security manager as they are repetitive in nature and do not enhance the security condition of the business.

There are other target activities that may have lower volumes of activity but require 24/7 operation such as firewall monitoring. In many firms, these activities may be performed on site during business hours and then may only be monitored by remote sensors after hours. Unfortunately, the intruders do not tend to keep the same hours as the business owners and, as a result, their activities often peak during the night.

Another candidate for outsourcing may be the specialized activities that take high degrees of skill and knowledge but are done very infrequently. Areas such as network design and security architecture may only need to be examined on a periodic basis in a company and having a fully trained resource on staff for those occasional needs may not be practical.

Cost information needed in an ROI calculation includes:

- Activity counts
- Timing per unit of activity
- Employee costs (salary, benefits, and other overhead costs)
- Activity-based cost (units × cost per unit of activity)
- Fixed costs
- Long-term costs (upgrades, software pricing)

Contract Issues for Security Outsourcing

All these cost figures are useful as the contract for the service that is outsourced will have to be compared and a gap analysis performed.

Usually as a part of that study, some differences will be observed between what has been done with internal resources and what services will be provided by the vendor. One area that is usually overlooked in the initial discussions is cost of changes to the system. Change management controls may be stricter with a vendor than would be otherwise true. Vendors typically have multiple clients sharing a server and a database, and making changes may impact other customers if they are not successful. Other areas to compare include cost of upgrades of hardware and software as well as management supervision costs on the part of the service provider.

The gray area is in the nonquantifiable benefits on both sides of this discussion. On the internal side, these will include familiarity with the business and understanding escalation policies that may not be written down. Other areas to look at are specialized services for key clients that an outside service provider may not be willing to perform as part of the contract. Some of these may be services that are unique to one business and are too specialized for a third party to offer as part of its services.

On the service provider side, there are also some nonquantifiable benefits. In information security, there can be a steep learning curve in spotting high-risk activities and reacting to them on a timely basis. A full-time 24/7 staff of experts will likely spot unusual activity faster than internal staff might. False-positive reports from alarms and audit systems create high additional cost to a business, and, again, the experts on staff at a service provider should be better at reacting to alerts and alarms and they should be able to spot anomalies faster due to their expertise. These experts also will see more real events and have a deeper understanding of activities and the correct way to react to them. In security incident response, time is of the essence, and if a full-time experienced person can reduce response time by an hour, it may be hard to quantify but could be very valuable.

Once the quantifiable and nonquantifiable benefits have been gathered, the next step is to make the comparison between the alternatives. This means trying to normalize some of the disparate terms and conditions between different vendors. It is not unusual to have vendors use very different terminology for two identical activities. For example, one vendor may describe watching logs and alerts on a firewall as "managing," while a different vendor may include rule changes and software patches in its firewall management offering and may have a separate price for firewall "monitoring." This type of analysis is an important part of the process and must be completed before a decision can be made on whether or not outsourcing an activity is practical.

Making a decision to outsource is not the endpoint of the process, as there are other management issues that may affect the decision and those should be part of the study.

Integration of Outsourcing with Internal Operational Functions

If an activity can be outsourced, it will not operate in a vacuum and those operations need to be integrated into the remaining business activities. There are several areas of overlap between a service provider and the client that should be reviewed prior to the outsourcing of the security processing. The key areas that the service provider and the client should work on are:

- *Security policy issues.* If e-mail filtering or firewall rules are part of the outsourcing agreement, there are policy decisions that need to be made by the customer and conveyed to the service provider for implementation. Examples of this include Web site filtering and which types of attachments are permissible with corporate e-mails. The outsourcing company should not be permitted to stop traffic without the prior approval of the customer. There are related issues regarding privacy and records retention that need to be included in this decision process.
- *Security monitoring.* Some managed security service providers can monitor devices that are on the client network and may not be directly part of the contract for managed security. The client needs to define any restrictions on the surveillance work that can be done by the service provider.
- *Interface with CSIRT.* The service provider can act on behalf of the client to perform forensics research on a security incident or can hold the material for study by the client. The interface between a service provider and the client's incident response team needs to be as seamless as possible, and the roles and responsibilities of each side should be clearly defined ahead of time.
- *Auditing.* The role of the client's internal and external auditors with respect to the work done by the service provider needs also to be resolved ahead of time. The auditor should have the right to validate the work of the service provider and have access to all client records and information.

The single biggest concern should be over the handling of security incidents and notification of any anomalies or events that have occurred that affect the client. Some service providers, particularly those that work in conjunction with ISPs, perform their duties with little or no interaction with the client or end user. They tend to see their work as protecting the ISP network and servers first and the client's information and applications second. As a result, they may not have a routine way of notifying clients about security incidents and actions until after the fact. It is up to the client to ask prior to signing a contract how this process will work as part of the due diligence activities.

This interaction can be of great concern to some businesses, particularly ones with well-developed security programs. In particular, the alerts and alarms received from a managed security provider (MSP) need to become part of the escalation policy for the information security management team. If the client has established a CSIRT, then the work of the managed security provider or other security outsourcer needs to be reviewed and become an integral part of the functions of the CSIRT. That is important as there may be multiple events occurring in a large network and there needs to be a central point of control and activity. The client needs to be in charge of the entire process and can delegate responsibilities as needed, but there should only be one group charged with managing the incident and formulating the action plan. That group may delegate certain tasks to others, but there needs to be a clear chain of command in this process.

Risks Associated with Outsourcing Security Functions

The number-one concern with outsourcing security functions, as expressed by security professionals is the perceived loss of control. Some businesses find it unacceptable to trust a third party with protecting their information assets and do not want to lose control of any part of their security duties. The earlier commentary on interfacing to a security incident response team describes an example of that type of concern in more depth.

Members of the security profession have expressed other concerns about the management and reaction to an incident that have to do with the speed of the response and what task can be delegated to the service provider. The most common example to cite is the reaction to a denial-of-service (DoS) attack, where a network node or Web site is maliciously flooded with bogus messages. Two of the choices of how to react are redirecting the messages to their point of origin and shutting off the affected node or server. If management delegates these actions, prior to taking action there needs to be a clear indication that the suspicious activity is actually occurring and is malicious in nature. If a third party redirects traffic and it goes to a site that has been hijacked by the perpetrator, there are some potential liability problems for the service provider and the client. Shutting down a node or server in error or having the shutdown cause other problems may also be sources of liability for the service provider. None of these actions should be taken lightly, and the consequences of these steps need to be understood ahead of time. That is one of the critical roles of management in making the decision about whether or not to outsource a security function.

Another risk has to do with the viability of the outsourcing company. This should come up during the due diligence investigation prior to contract execution, but the actual problem may crop up later after the contract is signed. In 2000–2002, a high number of managed security service providers went out of business, leaving their clients' networks exposed to risk until the connections could be moved to a new service provider. The client should have a written termination plan that is in place at the start of the contract and the client needs to monitor the well-being of the supplier and anticipate any problems that might occur.

Business Continuity Planning and Security Outsourcing

The business continuity plans of the service provider need to be reviewed as part of the due diligence process. The contingency plans in particular should be discussed, and there needs to be a clear understanding of how they will interface with the business continuity plans of the client. Some large service providers will have robust recovery plans that include near-instantaneous switching in the event of an outage. Others may have simpler plans that allow for periods of downtime or decreased service levels in the event of a disaster. That information should be disclosed and discussed prior to finalizing the contract. It is not sufficient to read the plan or a report by an auditor about the plan; the customer should review specific details of the plan and the impact on service levels and security. It should be absolutely unacceptable for security controls to be lowered during recovery from a disaster or service interruption. If anything, actions taken during an outage or interruption of service should face additional scrutiny. The control of access and system management functions should be at its highest level until the business has returned to normal.

The client needs to review all potential policy and procedural interfaces between its own operations and those of the service provider. Along with the contingency plans of the service provider, the security policies and safeguards should be reviewed and then matched to those of the client.

There are other risks associated with outsourcing that are similar to those with any technology project. The type of technology used by the outsourcing service provider must be stable and compatible with the client. Any major change in technology can affect both the functionality of the services provided and the ease of use of the business applications and services. Changes may also affect the interfaces with the client's networks and computers.

Other risks include those beyond the direct financial viability of the service provider such as mergers and acquisitions and changes in business plans and product mix. Any change in business plan may affect the quality and long-term functionality of the service.

The appeal of outsourcing should not be diminished because of the risks associated with it. All business plans have risk inherent in them, and the use of third-party service providers is no exception. The client's management has the ability and responsibility to manage those risks and ensure that its own plans have the right levels of internal and external services that will cost-effectively protect corporate assets.

Strategic Management Issues with Outsourced Security

Executive and senior management should be directly involved in the discussions on outsourcing security or the use of a managed security provider. This is a significant issue that needs to fit in with other strategic initiatives to be successful. There are a number of management issues that have already been mentioned that pertain to the operational aspects of outsourcing; all should be researched and the answers that are developed as part of that research need to be part of the final proposal.

There are still other strategic issues that will come forward as part of this process, and the answers to the questions raised will be part of the final decision process. Among the other strategic issues to be discussed is management's comfort with distributed control processes. In some firms, there is a strong desire to have a centralized command-and-control structure. It will be very hard for a firm with that type of culture to be comfortable with all the issues around outsourcing a controls function. Even though some of the tasks that can be outsourced are simple ones like firewall monitoring, this may be uncomfortable for a centralized structure to deal with on a regular basis, and that will doom the effort to fail in the long run.

Another area of concern should be the long-term growth plans of the prospective client. If the client firm plans to add significant levels of service or expand its market area, it will greatly affect outsourcing decisions and choices. Some well-respected security service providers are primarily local firms and their services may not scale well with a fast-growing client operation. International business and partners is another area that needs to be factored into this decision. The European Union, for example, has different work and privacy rules that will greatly affect the choice of security outsourcing venders for a company with a global operational footprint.

In the end, the decision to outsource any business function is not to be taken lightly; there are cultural, management control, financial, and operational issues that will enter into this decision. The short-term issues may also be different than the long-term ones. Some companies may find it favorable to outsource some security functionality in the short run while other business processes are undergoing change. It may then be appropriate to bring those same functions back in house at a later date when there is more stability in the business.

The decision criteria mentioned here are high-level choices, not technical ones. The technical decisions involved may actually be the easiest ones to make, and those can be delegated as part of the research effort. The higher-level decisions about long-term business strategy and vendor viability point out why this is such a significant decision and one that needs to have both the support and involvement of the executive management team at every step along the way. That is the best way to ensure a solid decision that will lead to goals that benefit the entire organization.

Chapter 16
Final Thoughts on Strategic Security

This book has covered a lot of material in pursuit of the ideas behind strategic security. A good question to ask at this point is why security is not a strategic value at more companies. Why do many security professionals still list management support as their number-one problem?

Perhaps this is due to two things. First, security is a complex problem. When someone is talking about information security, there are many areas he may be trying to cover in a single conversation, such as authentication services, risk management, viruses, and hackers. For some professionals the technical approach to security is the only way to look at the problem; others may disagree and want to talk about security policies and guidelines.

Privacy has become a focal point for a lot of these discussions, and the linkage between privacy and security, though clear to some people, is tenuous in the minds of others. Adding privacy to the already crowded discussion about information security may be adding confusion in the mind of some people in business.

The other major problem is that security does not have a good return on investment in the sense that business people think is important. They do understand the pain they might feel from a lack of security, but they do not see the benefits in the same light as they see other returns on investment. To them, investing in a new line of business will have a clearly identified rate of return, but spending money on security may not have any tangible benefits at all.

Both of these are daunting issues to overcome, but the goal of this book and others like it is to move this conversation further along with the full knowledge that there is not a single correct answer. It is important also to move the discussion up the organizational ladder and get it in the boardroom and the executive suite. Only if the executives understand these issues and comprehend their role in solving them will there be an end to the discussion. As business today becomes more global in reach and more dependent on technology, the executive management team needs to be fully involved in these discussions.

Executive Management and Security Management

At the outset of this chapter it was mentioned that the most common complaint of security professionals is not the difficulty of their job, but the perceived lack of support they feel for their position from senior management. To the security professional, this lack of support manifests itself in many ways. The Chief Security Officer, like most managers, has a long wish list of software and hardware. The budget requirements that all business executives deal with must apply to security budgets as well, but the security manager feels his role in loss prevention demands more attention than some other roles in the business. This is a challenge as the business managers too believe that additional funding would help them in their efforts, and it is up the executive management to choose between spending money on items that potentially enhance revenues or potentially prevent losses. It is not surprising that most executives choose revenue enhancement and will accept the risks from potential losses; after all, the rewards for senior executives are based on revenue and income generation as opposed to loss avoidance. The lack of support the security professional feels in those cases translates to growth and new markets, which can then increase the workload for the security manager, thus doubling his problem.

The lack of support is also directed to the cases where there are conflicts over policies. The security staff is usually the owner of the Information Security Policy manual and takes a proprietary view of policy. Sometimes the security manager will attempt to enforce policies across the board without any attempt to temper enforcement with judgment. That leads right into another favorite complaint of security professionals, which is a lack of enforcement of existing policies. Enforcement to the security manager includes penalizing the people who break the rules. Again, the executive managers look at security policies the same way they look at all policies and weigh the punishment with the crime. Access control violations are compared to violations of accounting policy and the myriad of other rules that exist in the workplace today. Enforcement may indeed be occurring, but without the level of severity or consistency that the security professional thinks is appropriate. Executive management has to weigh all types of policies with the other goals and objectives of the business.

This is not too different than the smaller decisions that must be made by the security managers regarding access controls and authorization. The security manager has to weigh the "need to know" against the "want to know," where the latter always requires greater access to information than the former.

The convergence of the decisions made by the executive manager and the security manager is in the balancing of their goals and objectives. One way to improve communication between the executive team and the security area is to link decisions made by both groups to find common goals and objectives and then work on the areas of disagreement.

Executive support is more than a letter from the CEO; support means that the objectives and goals of each group are shared. If there is agreement over goals and objectives, then there will be agreement over courses of action. That is the real test of support.

Another way to improve the situation is for both sides to open the pathway for better communication of their individual goals and projects. In the first chapter of this book, Choicepoint and Microsoft were singled out for their statements regarding their goals for security and privacy. Public statement of such goals is a good place to start. Such statements can then be used to form objectives and goals for the daily work of the business. The staff members working on a project can use those goals as templates for framing their decisions. There will always be points of contention and conflict, but if the goals are clearly stated, then they become a starting point to resolving conflict and moving on to more important tasks.

The Future of Information Security and the Challenges Ahead

Having placed the challenge of understanding the issues in the lap of the executive team, there are other questions to ask and problems to be raised. The challenges that lay ahead for the security professional are forcing him to think more strategically about his own job. In the past, the security professional had enough to do getting existing infrastructure protection schemes in place and managing the operational aspects of those systems. He had precious little time to think ahead and look at what would be the next threat to the enterprise. The difficulty with that approach is obvious. It is the old complaint about the military — you go into the next war with the weapons and tactics used to fight the last one. That never is a winning strategy.

What lies ahead are some technical and management challenges that will only make the job of securing the enterprise more difficult. Having said that, listing some of these challenges should help the executive to understand why it is so important to move beyond the tactical decision model to a strategic planning model for security. If it is important to have a strategic plan for growing a business, it should be as important to have a strategic plan for protecting the business.

Some of the challenges on the immediate horizon include:

- *Explosive growth in wireless networks.* McDonald's and Starbucks are already rolling out wireless access points as a service to their customers. More and more people are installing wireless networks in their homes. That creates a real challenge to the security professional as people have become accustomed to routinely moving information between home and office. Wireless communication will add to the problem of secure communications and to the challenge of protecting the privacy of individuals and their information.

- *Homeland Security.* There are a lot of unknowns facing business as a result of what has become a global fight on terrorism. In the United States, the creation of the Department of Homeland Security has signaled a new direction in the way government views security and information. This has led to a number of new initiatives that have yet to be tested in court. This will be a very challenging area in the coming years as security policies and procedures will be coming under more direction and guidance from the federal government.
- *Privacy.* Like the challenges from Homeland Security, privacy is a growing concern that has a lot of unknowns associated with it. Privacy issues and privacy management are in their infancy, but this is a rapidly growing area. The current approach of disclosure statements is cumbersome. There is also a problem of measuring the effectiveness of relying on disclosures of sources and uses of information. There are some recent complaints that information has been obtained illegally from third-party brokers that may cause changes in how businesses obtain information and what assurances they can rely on that their sources have a legal right to sell information. Many businesses will first turn to their information security staff to deal with privacy issues as security and privacy are linked together in the minds of most people. It will be up to the security professional to monitor those rules and see that there are appropriate mechanisms in place to protect the security and privacy of information.
- *Copyright protection.* This is another growing and very challenging area that affects business. This started out several years ago with the monitoring of software licenses and the tracking of software registration. Now it is evolving into new and uncharted territory. One group, led by software vendors, wants the ability to monitor customers' servers to look proactively for pirated copies of software. Another group, led by the music industry, wants to employ private business in tracking down music pirates through the monitoring of network traffic and server activity. Both groups have a sympathetic ear in most businesses as the executive managers understand their complaint and understand the need to fight piracy and the resulting loss of revenue. On the other hand, there is reluctance by individuals and businesses to let a third party monitor internal IT assets. This issue, hopefully, will be resolved by technological changes in the way software and music is distributed, but until that time comes, it will be a problem that will involve security professionals and business owners.
- *Auditing.* The Sarbanes–Oxley Act in the United States has forced management to personally certify the accuracy of financial reports

and information. Management can only be comfortable in doing so if it can trust the integrity of those systems and the people who support them. The fundamental test of integrity is that the information has not been altered or changed by unauthorized means, which makes this an information security issue. As executive management begins to understand the importance of its certification statements, it will also want more and more assurances from its security staff that information systems have the proper safeguards in place.

- *Device convergence.* Consumers are leading the charge to use devices that are multi-functional. This means using cell phones that do text messaging and can send and receive e-mail. Convergence includes the tablet PCs that are similar to personal digital assistants but much more powerful and have more capabilities for communication. Even something as simple today as a realtor's lock box can make use of digital information that tracks who looked at a house and how much time they spent inside. Device convergence also leads back to the convergence of security and privacy concerns.

- *Radio frequency identification.* RFID is another example of an emerging technology that will have an impact on information security and privacy. This is a system that allows manufacturers to place electronic tags on merchandise that can replace bar coding for inventory control and pricing. The tags can be read by a scanner, even when the merchandise is in a closed box. A concern has already been expressed by watchdog groups that the tags could be intentionally left on the merchandise to allow vendors to track items after they have been sold. This is another example of a physical security device that has implications for privacy and the information security profession.

- *Threats to encryption technology.* Some experts believe that the current crop of encryption algorithms will be useless in less than ten years. In that timeframe, experts at HP and other leading-edge firms see the possibility that quantum computing and other breakthrough technologies will make it possible to crack encrypted messages in hours or minutes using simple brute-force guessing as opposed to the days and weeks that it takes today. If the current encryption algorithms become insecure or unreliable, new ways must be found to protect information.

- *Global workforce.* The continued globalization of the economy is a blessing and a curse. It opens up new markets for products and also makes it possible to harness the intellect of people in other countries. It also means that communications channels have to pass through multiple countries that have different rules and legal systems. It also means that more information will be flowing through the Internet than ever before, and that information is increasingly valuable and therefore a target for illegal activity.

- *Mobile workers.* All that new technology is also creating a mobile workforce at the local level. More and more companies use hoteling as a basic office strategy. In hoteling, people do not have a permanent location, but can sign in at any office in any city and expect to be 100 percent productive instantly. That puts real stress on designing flexible networks and being creative in authenticating users. It also presents challenges for securing networks and network access points.

These trends and ideas will be surpassed by others in a short time. Those as-yet-unknown technologies will bring with them new risks and new challenges to the security profession. Only through linking themselves to the business owners who are driving these changes can a security program hope to be successful. The security profession must stay on top of emerging issues and constantly search for new ways to cost effectively do its job.

There will always be exceptions to the rules. It is a big marketplace. Some companies will continue to be successful using older technology and working in a more traditional manner. Today, there are still many places that are primarily using manual processes in place of more costly automated solutions. This will always be the case, but the exceptions should not provide a justification to ignore progress. It is important to look ahead and anticipate the changes that are coming. Looking ahead to the future, though, is only part of what it means to be strategic. It is also important to make sure the entire organization is in step with the changes and that everyone is on board with the plans to move forward. Security has to be a willing partner in this effort. Security professionals cannot wait to make things perfect; instead, they also have to learn the business and help things move forward in a secure manner. That will involve compromise and negotiation skills that are part of the skill set of strategic managers.

The last part of the definition of strategic security is to have a mission that is worthy of the name. It is not enough to simply state that security and privacy are important goals. The mission must be up to the challenge of providing leadership in how those goals are to be achieved. The business manager will set lofty goals and have challenging aspirations. The security manager must learn that those goals are his goals too, but his job is to ensure the goals are met with a minimum of risk. That is the real challenge of defining strategic security.

Appendix
Helpful Internet Resources

General Security Web Sites

InfraGard (FBI and business security partnership program)
www.infragard.net

National Infrastructure Protection Center
www.nipc.gov

Carnegie Mellon CERT
www.cert.org

International Information Systems Security Certification Consortium (ISC²)
www.isc2.org

Information Systems Audit and Control Association Foundation (ISACA)
www.isaca.org

Georgia Stop Identity Theft
www.stopidentitytheft.org

Homeland Defense Journal
www.homelanddefensejournal.com

Information Systems Security Association
www.issa.org

The Johns Hopkins University Information Security Institute (ISI)
www.jhuisi.jhu.edu

These represent good resources to use as accompanying material to that presented in this book. These sites are vendor neutral and have a wealth of information.

Index

C

R

S